THIS
GRACE
GIVEN

◆

David H. C. Read

With best wishes from
the author,

David Read

July 1986.

WILLIAM B. EERDMANS PUBLISHING COMPANY
GRAND RAPIDS, MICHIGAN

Contents

To Rory, now fifteen—
and his generation

Introduction

Autobiographies have long been among my favorite books, and because I have read so many of them, I am aware of the difficulties and dangers of this kind of self-revelation. In the first place, there seems to be an element of vanity in the assumption that one's own life experiences should be of interest to anyone beyond a few relatives and friends. There are indeed autobiographies that are little more than exercises in egotism, profiles of self-importance for public relations purposes that drop all the right names, but these are few and are soon remaindered. The fact is that we are all engaged in autobiography every time we open our mouths or write a letter. We are sharing our experiences, our opinions, our memories, and our hopes with one another as human beings making the same mysterious journey through life. Just as there are self-serving autobiographies, so there are bores who never stop talking about themselves. ("Sir," said Dr. Johnson to Boswell, "you have but two topics, yourself and me. I am sick of both.") A genuine autobiography is a contribution, however slight, to the universal discourse, and our natural curiosity about one another makes it welcome.

The difficulty with this kind of writing for one whose normal occupation is writing for publication—whether as a novelist, a critic, a journalist, or even a preacher—is that it requires an effort to detach oneself from the attitude of an observer, commentator, or expositor and to set down as simply and directly as possible what comes from the heart about one's own experiences and reflections. A novelist has to guard against over-dramatizing when creating characters, against letting a skill in fiction varnish the truth. A critic has to overcome the temptation to regard his own life as a drama on which to comment. A journalist must find it hard not to do a professional job of reporting the personal experiences he is recalling. And a preacher has to refrain from a notorious tendency "to point a moral, or adorn a tale." An autobiography demands candor and the kind of sincerity that follows when two close friends are talking.

Yet, the fact that this self-revelation is meant for a much wider audience than an intimate friend must surely mean that limits should be imposed on such candor. Surely there is a place for reticence, that rare quality that has become unfashionable. The tendency today (to use a phrase that is as ugly as the practice) is "to let it all hang out." Advertisements lure the reader with expectations that someone's life story "reveals all," and promise the kind of intimate detail that is not normally talked about at all. Reticence is not demanded simply because every human being has the right to an inner sanctum that is not open to public inspection, but because of the inevitable repercussions for the people whose names are liberally sprinkled throughout a certain kind of autobiography. The great autobiographies are masterpieces despite their reluctance to divulge intimate details, just as the great biographies are lasting works of art without delving into personal minutiae.

Art is inevitably selection. And the art of autobiography demands some theme to control that selection. The writer of the Fourth Gospel was aware as he finished his book that he had made a selection of the deeds and words of Jesus, and that selection was dictated by his theme. "There were indeed," he wrote, "many other signs that Jesus performed in the presence of his disciples, which are not recorded in this book." Later a postscript adds, "There is much else that Jesus did. If it were all to be recorded in detail I suppose the whole world could not hold the books that would be written." If that sounds to you like a pious exaggeration, reflect on the paper and ink that would be required to record in detail everything that you did or said or thought during the last twenty-four hours. If you complain that selecting a theme makes a book tendentious, the answer must be that of course it does, for that word of recent ill-repute simply means that the writer has a bias, a tendency to select with a purpose. Don't we all have a bias? Aren't we all driven by some purpose when we express ourselves in writing—even if the purpose is to indicate that there is no purpose worth having and no meaning to be found in the daily round?

The theme that controls the selection of events in this book is one man's experience of God. I am trying to discover what it is in my experience of life that has led me to the kind of belief in God and the Gospel of Christ that I am aware of today, and what it may have been that made me not only a believer but one committed to sharing that belief through the ministry of the Church. By relating this story I hope to encourage others to discern the presence of God in their own life story. Surely it is possible to have such a purpose and still be candid, to be selective and yet honest.

My gratitude goes to the very many people, beyond those mentioned in these pages, who have been ministers of grace to me. A special note of thanks is due to my secretary, Carolyn Mathis, who has labored with her usual skill and devotion in the preparation of this manuscript.

U_{nto} *me,*
who am less than the least of all saints,
is this grace given,
that I should preach among the Gentiles
the unsearchable riches of Christ.

—*EPHESIANS 3:8*

THIS
GRACE
GIVEN

Chapter One

THE GOD
IN OUR
GENES

One wintry afternoon in the late nineteen-forties I was driving in my ramshackle open car from Edinburgh to St. Andrews, where I had an engagement at the university. After crossing the Firth of Forth I was soon in the vicinity of Cupar, the capital of the county of Fife, which happens to be my birthplace. ("Happens to be"? The cliché slipped out. Does anything just happen to be? Since the point of these reflections is the search for the directing presence of God, I should avoid this expression, which really conceals a popular pagan philosophy of sheer chance, the goddess of Fortune. Do you just happen to be here now?) It is only eight miles from Cupar to St. Andrews, but I was not altogether sure of the way. To add to my confusion it was growing dark, and soon great clouds of mist came rolling in from the North Sea. By the time I was a mile or two beyond Cupar I was totally lost. Peering through and over the windshield, I caught sight of an ancient signpost and pulled over to the side of the road. As I stood for a moment looking around, a curious feeling swept over me. As far as I could see through the mist, I was stranded on a bleak stretch of moorland, and there was not a sound, not a trace of a human being or even an animal. Yet I sensed what I can only call a Presence, not exactly spooky but vaguely disturbing. There are quite a few places in Scotland where this seems to happen. In fact, someone had recently remarked to me that the island of Iona is a "thin" place, and I knew what he was referring to—places where the barrier between the seen and the unseen worlds seems to be stretched thin. In this mood I peered up at the signpost. Then I understood. It read MAGUS MOOR.

One evening in 1679 a party of Covenanters came riding across this moor led by David Haxton of Rathillet, from whom I have inherited my first two names. At that time the Covenanters were the followers of Presbyterian leaders who had entered into a covenant, signed at the Kirk of the Greyfriars in Edinburgh, to resist the imposition of episcopacy in Scotland by edict of the king. The point at issue was not so much a matter of doctrine, a style of worship, or even church government as it was the freedom of the church from the control of the state. In this the Covenanters were ahead of their time. As a result of their defiance of the Crown, some bloody wars were fought. In the north of Fife the fiercest opponent and persecutor of the Covenanters was Archbishop Sharp of St. Andrews. Thus, when Haxton and his armed followers were crossing Magus Moor, they were surprised and delighted when the archbishop's coach suddenly came rumbling out of the mists. With a shout of "The Lord hath delivered him into our hands!" the Covenanters drew their swords and surrounded the coach. Robert Louis Stevenson has described how at this point Haxton sat silent on his horse and waited while Sharp crawled over on his hands and knees to beg for his life. Thereupon Haxton is reported to have said, "I will lay no hand on you—either to kill or to save you"—a claim of dubious neutrality that I admit has haunted me on certain occasions. The archbishop was quickly dispatched, and the Covenanters went on their way. The wars went on with varying fortunes until finally, at the Battle of Rullion Green, the royal forces prevailed, and Haxton, among others, was taken prisoner. He was accused of complicity in Sharp's murder, found guilty, and then hanged, drawn, and quartered in the Grassmarket at Edinburgh. His body thus lies buried in four different places in Scotland.

Since Haxton had no children, I cannot claim direct ancestry, but my maternal grandmother was a Haxton, and the Haxtons of Rathillet usually had a David in the family, thus preserving the name. Curiously, my maternal grandfather, David Carswell, came into possession of Rathillet, and that is where my mother was raised. Having thus explained the mystery of the middle names, I am free to wonder about this particular strain in my ancestry, and you, if you like, to speculate on my genetic heritage.

Since there is always a furious argument raging among philosophers, scientists, anthropologists, and theologians about the relative influences of heredity and environment, nature and nurture, freedom and determinism, let me say that, like David Haxton on Magus Moor, I have always found it impossible to come down decisively on one side or the other. I am sure that we all inherit certain character traits, a kind of bias of disposition, from our ancestors, just as a vulnerability to certain diseases can be hereditary. Yet I am equally sure that we are not enslaved by our genes. So it is with our early environment. It has a tremendous effect on our character, but everyone knows that twins living in an identical environment in their early years can develop in quite different ways, and that there are many examples of men and women who have triumphed over the worst possible childhood conditions. In any case, it is impossible to determine just when the influence of heredity stops and that of one's environment takes over. Which has the greater influence on the baby in the womb? And where does God come in? If we find, on reflection, that he has been active in providing us with good parents and a reasonably happy early environment, shouldn't we also think of him as active in the limbo of our ancestry? Conversely, if we had irresponsible parents and a childhood for which we would honestly rather blame than praise this God, would it not be natural to curse him for endowing us with a horrific set of genes? All I can say is that I have been conscious— increasingly so as I grow older—of the pressures exerted on me by forces that can be traced back through my childhood to the mysterious influence of ancestry. And at the same time I am aware that none of these pressures from within is irresistible, none relieves me of the responsibility to choose rightly according to what I believe to be the will of God. To know a little about our ancestry may help us at times to recognize a bias, to guard against what you might call a "family failing," but those who know little or nothing of their forebears are in no way at a disadvantage in meeting life's challenges. I tend to think now that we make too much of the influence of heredity, since nearly everybody is inclined to idealize one's ancestors. When I hear anyone who is considering adopting a child worrying about possible sinister hereditary strains, I point out that all of us undoubtedly have crooks and criminals of all kinds among the thousands of our forebears.

Like most other people, I have wondered at times about the question of reincarnation. Has the stream of genes been interrupted at certain points by our appearance in quite another role? And how does God fit into *this* picture? Has he been taking me out of and sending me back to this mortal existence over millions of years, and is the whole process designed to produce, in the end, the kind of being he wants me to be? Let me just offer a comment or two before I get back to my grandparents. The doctrine of reincarnation has attracted far more adherents than those of the religions that teach it. It has found some support among Christian theologians, from Origen in the early days of the Church to one or two in our own times. My old friend Geddes MacGregor has just published a vigorous book in its defense called *The Christening of Karma*, and I keep meeting people, usually rather loosely attached to the Church, who are quite sure that they have been here before. I have two comments. The first is that, just as we tend to idealize our ancestors, so many people see themselves in previous incarnations as pharaohs, philosophers, military commanders, and bishops, but few imagine they were slaves, cavemen, menials in the castle kitchens, or foot soldiers in Napoleon's army. The other is that in my search for the City of God, in my response to what I perceive as his grace, and in my resistance of temptation, I am not at all helped by the thought that I may now be expiating some sin of a previous incarnation or enjoying the reward of an exemplary life as a horse in ancient Greece. If, like most of us, I have no knowledge whatever of my past incarnations, how can I derive any benefit from such experiences? If God is in this process, would he not let me know?

But is God in any sense active in our ancestry as a factor to be reckoned with today? The Bible certainly suggests a positive answer. As one gets older, the constant references to religious roots—"the God of Abraham, Isaac, and Jacob," "the God of our father," "the rock whence we were hewn"—take on more meaning. In our youth we are naturally impatient with what sounds like religious nostalgia, and sometimes we reach our sixties or seventies before developing a lively interest in our great-grandparents. "Faith of our Fathers" is apt to be sung more lustily by the older half of any congregation. For me the realization that God has been at work in my life has been continually pushed back to earlier times. When, in my late teens, God became central and compelling to me as I experienced the call of Christ through the activities of a group of contemporaries (and underwent a kind of conversion experience), I was inclined to sweep aside any thought of his influence upon me through my parents, let alone my ancestors. I was then one of the religious "Now Generation" and behaved as though God had just suddenly burst into my life. Later I began to realize that such things as infant prayers, church services, and surely my baptism had something to do with God's concern for my life. Now, when I hear the psalmist declare in a magnificent poetic outburst, "My substance was not hid from thee, when I was made in secret, and curiously wrought in the lowest parts of the earth. Thine eyes did see my substance, yet being imperfect; and in thy book all my members were written . . . ," I have indeed a sense of what John Calvin would call the "prevenience" of God, and trace that back through the centuries of my ancestors.

However, the vast number of these ancestors is really beyond my comprehension. (As a boy I was always puzzled—and sometimes I still am—by how the roll of my forebears multiplied—two parents, four grandparents, eight great-grandparents, and so on into the billions—and yet had to end up with a single couple, whether Adam and Eve or a couple of apes.) Since I know very little about genetics, I don't know if there is some statute of limitations for the activities of genes, but it has occurred to me that my ancestors, and yours, must at one time all have been Roman Catholics, and before that possibly some kind of Druids. So I must guess at what God has given me through my roots by confining myself to the more immediate forebears of whom I have some kind of information or memories.

This brings me back to the Haxtons, the Carswells, the Brodies, and the Martins on my mother's side, and the Reads and Macreas of my father's line. Since it was the Scottish side (my mother was *very* Scottish while my father was *very* "northern Ireland") that was the major influence in my early days, I have to think about that strain of Scottish Presbyterianism that was probably the strongest part of my religious heritage, and try to reach it through early memories of David Carswell, my grandfather, who had left Rathillet by the time I came to know him. He had a farm in Fife that rejoiced in the name of Blacketyside, and he lived there with his wife, Annie Brodie, who had married him at the age of seventeen. Since World War I broke out when I was four and my brother was six, and my father spent most of these war years in Flanders as a machine gunner with the Black Watch regiment, my brother and I spent a good deal of time with relatives, and as a consequence we were closer to the previous generation than children usually are. We went to school only intermittently and spent a lot of time running free at Blacketyside and in the company of assorted uncles, aunts, and cousins—all, of course, Presbyterians with varying degrees of enthusiasm for the ministrations of the Church of Scotland.

From my brief narrative of the adventures of David Haxton, you might expect that the ancestral religion I encountered would be the stern, strict, and occasionally ferocious brand of Calvinism familiar to us in popular caricatures. It was nothing of the sort. The God who emerged from these early surroundings was to me clearly one to be respected. He was one of whom even my formidable—and often irascible—Grandfather Carswell evidently stood in awe. I believe that I sensed something of what my theological mentor John Baillie once described—how as a child he knew that, just as he was subject to his parents' will, they also were subject to the will of a Higher Power. But for me there was nothing at all terrifying about this God in whom my ancestors believed.

My grandfather had a habit of using an expletive, a short Scottish monosyllable—"Cugh!" When I tried this out in my own way, my mother reproved me with the startling information that this was just another way of saying "God." I remember wondering whether this was what was meant by "taking God's name in vain," and therefore why it was wrong for me but all right for my grandfather. Another vividly remembered snatch of conversation comes back to me—this from a mealtime discussion (like most children, I was all ears at the adult dining-table). The subject of debate was whether it was possible to read a passage aloud and be thinking of something else. My grandfather had smiled into his beard and remarked, "You get an example of that every Sunday night"—that being the time when he conducted family prayers and read from the big Bible on the shelf.

My eighteenth- and nineteenth-century ancestors were, on the whole, members of the majority party in the Church of Scotland, a group who had greatly modified the rigors of an earlier Calvinism and were by no means averse to the amenities, or hostile to the culture, of the surrounding world. These Moderates, as they came to be called, were devoted to the established Church, generally conservative in both politics and religion, "God-fearing" in the sense in which we apply that word to a Washington or a Lincoln, upholders of a strong morality of honesty, fidelity, and trust, and averse to anything that smacked of fanaticism. (Henry Raeburn's portrait *The Skating Parson*, which has recently been featured on a popular Christmas card, represents the type—assured of their religion and their place in contemporary society, elegantly balanced between the skeptics and the fanatics, the worldly and the otherworldly.) The first pastoral visit I can remember is not that of a devout cleric summoning us all to kneel in prayer; what I recall is a hurried glimpse one winter afternoon of my grandfather raising a glass and saying, "Your health, sir" to a venerable figure in a black coat and a clerical collar. Since it was the first time my brother and I had heard the expression, we repeated it for days as we raised our mugs of milk.

My Scots grandmother gave me the impression that this was a difficult but essentially fascinating world and opened up to us boys the land of romance and wonder. She was a superb teller of fairytales, from Hans Christian Andersen to the brothers Grimm, and—what we enjoyed even more—of the exploits of a daredevil brother of hers who got into all kinds of scrapes and adventures. Eventually, of course, he founded a Brodie family on this side of the Atlantic. She bowed her head at table when my grandfather mumbled his incomprehensible grace (the only words that came through to me were "Gracious God . . . pardon sins . . . bless our mercies [he *couldn't* have said that] . . . glorious Christ"), and she seemed to enjoy taking us to church in spite of our reluctance to walk two miles in kilted outfits with stiff, starched collars. She didn't talk to us about God; she simply conveyed a religion that was sure, obligatory, and fundamentally happy.

But my grandmother did have a sister whom we came to call our "religious aunt." Aunt Bella, the widow of a lawyer in Brechin in Angus, was short, stout, and to my mind forever recalled Queen Victoria. Since we visited her for weeks at a time, it was difficult to avoid God in her home. There were morning and evening prayers, and at least one complete service on Sundays, when I remember spending the sermon-time slowly turning my gloves inside out and back again, believing that when the operation had been performed three times the sermon *must* come to an end. The atmosphere of her home was pervaded by the memories of one of her sons, who had died at the age of six. On rainy days we were allowed to play with *his* toys, and we were regularly provided with the kind of improving books with which he had been supplied. My chief memory of these books is of the lurid-colored pictures of such bloody episodes as David's fight with Goliath and Daniel's night in the lions' den. This was another side of my ancestral religion, and I wasn't sure that I liked it. Yet I was getting an impression of a God who was both mysterious and kind, and who seemed still to care for that little cousin who had died. Aunt Bella belonged to the Free Church that had seceded from the Church of Scotland in 1843 and had taken a more evangelical, independent line. With all its austerities, it conveyed a strong sense of a people for whom Christ was very near and very helpful. Its God was, I dimly felt, a little more challenging, and perhaps a little more exciting, than the dignified but rather distant God of the "Auld Kirk." But he seemed to me a little too easily shocked.

There was another figure from this Free Church tradition who looms large in my memory, although his visits were rare. He was my Uncle Bob, a civil engineer from Briston, England, who had designed important bridges and stretches of railway line. Whenever we were anticipating his arrival at Blackety-side, there was always a sense that something important was about to happen. My mother would explain to us that he was a celebrated civil engineer, a figure in local politics, and an elder in the Free Church, "but," she would add in hushed tones, "he is a liberal, and we don't want him talking politics with your grandfather." To me it sounded a little like that verse in the Bible that says, "Now Naaman, captain of the host of the king of Syria, was a great man with his master. . . . He was a mighty man in valor, *but he was a leper.*" I didn't really know what a liberal was, but I felt that the great Uncle Bob must have blotted his copybook somewhere along the line. In retrospect, I see him as one representative of God-fearing ancestors whose blood must be flowing in my veins. At least I learned from him that there is more than one way of interpreting what God wants us to do in the realm of politics, a truth that has not waned with the passing years.

I should also mention my Aunt Margaret, my mother's youngest sister. She was entrusted with our education when numerous childhood illnesses kept us from attending the local school. She was enterprising, essentially rebellious, and given to strong likes and dislikes. For my mother she was often a thorn in the flesh. Whenever we were away from home and a letter from her arrived, I recognized the handwriting and waited for an explosion from my mother. It nearly always took the same form: "Baggage!"—a word I associate with my late aunt to this day. A few of Aunt Margaret's "foibles" revealed that conservative genes are not invincible in any family. For one thing, she was what was then called a suffragette. Women's right to vote seems an elementary thing today, but then it was a battle, sometimes literally to the death. One of my earliest recollections of my hometown is hearing about suffragettes burning down the local hall. So it came about that these brave ladies entered my private chamber of horrors, the other chief inmates being black cats. (I adored cats by day but was terrified of them by night. In later years my mother told me that I would wake up screaming "Pussycats crawling over me; suffragettes bothering me!")

Every summer my family—even when my father was away at the front—made a pilgrimage to his home in the little town of Pettigo, which lies on the county lines of Fermanagh and Donegal in Ireland, and is consequently now half in Ulster and half in the Republic. My Scots-Irish ancestors came to this area during what were known as the "plantations" in Ulster in the early seventeenth century. This immigration, of course, contributed to the present tragic divisions in Ireland—although I confess that today, whenever I see the slogan "England, get out of Ireland," I wonder if the suggestion is that there should be a mass uprooting of families that have been in Ireland for hundreds of years longer than any Irish have been in America. (The Scots may be excepted from this war cry, since they tended to be against the English establishment and sometimes made common cause with Roman Catholics as Irish nationalists.)

There was, however, no doubt at all about the Protestant and loyalist genes of my Irish ancestors. We still have in the family an old table made from the wood of the gates of Londonderry, which were slammed in the face of King James' troops before the famous siege. Whatever religion they brought with them from the southwest of Scotland, it soon was identified with the religion of William of Orange, and I have a vivid recollection of my grandfather presenting me with the munificent gift of half a crown on the anniversary of the Battle of the Boyne. Some of my memories are of the "Troubles," as they were called, the armed rebellion of the Sinn Feiners in the twenties. The republican forces invaded and captured Pettigo in 1921, and some Protestant farmers were assassinated. That summer I read on the wall near my grandparents' home words that are familiar still today—"Up the I.R.A.: long live the Republic"—with a crude drawing underneath of a revolver and a coffin. The fighting continued and British troops recaptured the town. So the following year the wall had been whitewashed, and on it appeared the picture of William of Orange crossing the Boyne, with the words "Fear God and honor the King."

I mention these incidents to make clear how religion and politics are strongly intertwined in my heritage, and how from Haxton of Rathillet to the ancestors who defended Londonderry there can be no doubt of the militant Protestant heritage that is inevitably mine. It might seem foreordained that I would be swayed to one particular way of worshiping God and one inevitable interpretation of the Christian gospel. But that is not by any means the whole story. So let me introduce you to my paternal grandfather and grandmother.

Robert Read, when I knew him, was the patriarch of the little town. He had written its history, and he knew and loved its inhabitants, both Protestant and Catholic. He was a farmer who ran the local post-office and general store as well. He was also a great reader and raconteur. In his early days he had twice circled the globe in sailing ships, and so could tell enthralling tales of adventure. When he died in his ninetieth year, everyone in the community, whatever his or her religion or social status, turned out to honor him. But for me and my dawning awareness of my ancestors' religion, the important matter was that here was my image of God. We all know the cliché that portrays God as an old man with a benevolent face and a long white beard—and that is exactly what my Grandfather Read looked like. Sitting at the head of the table, he would lead a sparkling conversation that was, to the consternation of my mother, often interrupted with glee or exuberant laughter; and when I chanced to catch his eye, he would nod and smile in a way that aroused in me a feeling of infinite respect and love. There was nothing in the least harsh or unbending about the religion he represented for me. He was raised in the Church of Ireland and, I now suspect, loved the cadences of the Book of Common Prayer. My mother, who always found the Irish ways of my father's family—with their love of funny stories and practical jokes and their penchant for exaggeration—somewhat alien to her Scottish no-non-sense mind and passion for the exact truth, used to confide in my brother and me, "Your Grandfather Read is a *good* man"—the highest tribute in her vocabulary.

My Irish grandmother was for me yet another representative of religion. She was a strong-minded Methodist—so strong-minded that she had persuaded her husband to come to her church rather than the other way around. She was tough, hardworking, and intolerant of any deviation from the behavior she firmly believed God expected of us. One Sunday afternoon I was idly whittling a piece of wood when she sharply asked me what I was doing.

"I'm making a boat," I replied innocently.

"They must be hard up for boats if they have to be made on the Sabbath," she shot back grimly—and I went away disconsolate.

I suppose that conversation, which I remember verbatim, must have roused in me some rebellious thoughts about a God who wouldn't tolerate a little boy whittling on Sunday. At least it taught me that God, whose reality I never doubted for a moment, didn't always give grown-ups identical instructions. My grandfather's God wouldn't have minded about that little boat.

It was in Pettigo that I had my first experience of Sunday school, which my brother and I attended with our cousins. My chief recollection of this, I have to confess, is my experiment of tying together the pigtails of the little girls in the row in front of me. I have no memory of what was said about God, although in the literature provided, which I read avidly on our return home, I remember vividly the assertion that if I set up a great chest in my room and asked God to fill it with gold coins, he wouldn't do it. That piece of ancestral wisdom stayed with me, and was a strong theological strand in my later experiments with prayer.

If all these tales about my immediate ancestors seem to lead to the conclusion that I was foreordained to be a believer rather than an unbeliever, a Protestant rather than a Catholic, a Presbyterian rather than a Methodist, and a preacher rather than a stockbroker, let me say flatly that I don't believe it. I do believe that there are currents within us that may be pushing us in one direction or another, but they are so varied and their influence so easily countered that I flatly reject any theory of genetic determinism. But I am enough of a Calvinist to believe that God was in my past, already calling me and offering me his grace, just as I believe that he was in your past, and that he has given us our varied heredity for his own mysterious purposes.

Chapter Two

GROWING UP
WITH
GOD

In thinking back on my childhood, I find it hard to disentangle genuine recollections from those that are trimmed and shaped by the passage of time and by theories I've absorbed from other books and other people. A curtain of ideas, woven from biographies, autobiographies, theological doctrines, psychological interpretations, and conversations with relatives and friends, hangs between me *now* and what was actually happening to me *then*. The effect is to make me suspect that some of the memories I shall be dredging up as evidence of "growing up with God" may be distorted by subsequent convictions that this is how it *must* have happened or, worse, that this is how it *ought* to have happened. These are the hazards in any effort to reach the truth that lies somewhere behind the memory.

I seem to have been aware very early of this problem. For I do distinctly—yes, *distinctly*—remember coming up with a subtle theory about it when I was about five years old. I was playing a game of "Do you remember when?" with my brother and suggested that neither he nor I was really remembering but only recalling remembering. Each year, as it were, a certain memory was passed on, but it was impossible to actually remember the original event. This theory has surprising ramifications. I suppose a psychiatrist might say that the form in which a memory is crystallized in the mind is quite as important as the exact truth about what happened. A poet might play around with the idea of what this does to "emotion recollected in tranquillity." A New Testament form critic would naturally draw conclusions about the transmission of the actual words and deeds of Jesus before anything was written down. Philosophers would be tempted to see in this progressive dimming of the memory some support for Plato's theory that we arrive in this world complete with all necessary knowledge, and that therefore all subsequent education is the literal "drawing out" of what was already there.

Examples of this shaping of the memory are not difficult to discover, and I find that my own religious recollections have been influenced by later experiences and interests. For instance, in a period of what I could call my "precocious piety," when prayer was very real to me, I would tend to magnify memories of what looked like supernatural intervention in my own affairs. Later, at a time when religion had become little more than a conventional backdrop to my life, I reinterpreted these memories or else they vanished from my mind. Then in my "skeptical adolescent" period they seemed, when I thought about them at all, to be the kind of incidents that would have made great sport for writers like George Bernard Shaw, D. H. Lawrence, Aldous Huxley, and Mark Twain. Later still, when under the spell of the Romantic poets, I'm sure my early religious memories got a Wordsworthian twist, influenced by lines like these:

> Not in entire forgetfulness,
> And not in utter nakedness,
> But trailing clouds of glory do we come
> From God, who is our home.

If I had written this book during that period, my earliest religious memories would probably have come to you "trailing" some of these "clouds of glory." And if I had written this book during the following period—a time when I combined a delight in Augustan clarity and order with passionately orthodox Christian conviction—I would have filtered these memories through a very different sieve and presented them as compelling evidence for the truth of the gospel. Let me just say, then, that my tales of "growing up with God" are offered now, with all due reservations, as very real and powerful memories that I have no desire either to suppress or to exploit, and that help me to understand both who I am and what and why I believe.

I suppose childhood prayers are, for most of us, the earliest key to any experience of "growing up with God," and one I remember is a verse from one of Wesley's hymns:

> Gentle Jesus, meek and mild,
> Look upon a little child;
> Pity my simplicity,
> Suffer me to come to thee.

I associate these words with bedtime and warm milk, with a turned-down lamp or flickering candle, and with the reassuring presence of my mother as we faced the adventure of another night. The routine of prayer was snuggled somewhere between the protests or the tired acceptance of bed, and the giggles and squabbles that would follow until sleep came. It's tempting to think, as I look through the prism of later reflections, that I raised all kinds of questions about the sense of talking to Somebody who was totally invisible (as well as incomprehensible); that I demanded an explanation of every line I was expected to repeat (for years I construed "Pity my simplicity" as "Pity me some plicity" and wondered idly what plicity could be); and that I raised a query about that odd word "bless," which figured in my supplications following the hymn verse. ("God bless Daddy and Mummy and Bob. God bless granddaddies, grandmummies, uncles, aunts, cousins, and all my dear friends"—I remember those words verbatim and also the curious and exciting additions that crept in after August 4, 1914. "God bless the Belgians, the Serbians"—I *know* I mentioned them, although I can't remember all the people I prayed for as the war got more complicated.) But I don't think I had any such worries about these prayers. Certainly I had no theological questions about the petition that entered our prayers and stayed in them for four long years: "Make the war stop soon." All the questions flooded in later; at the time I found the whole operation perfectly natural and acceptable. It never occurred to me that millions of boys and girls might end a day with biscuits and a bath, but no prayer—or even with no biscuits or bath.

What I am sure I sensed at this time was the existence of some power that was greater than my father's, greater even than the king's—and, fortunately, much greater than that of the kaiser, the bogeyman who then haunted British children. There was something special about this contact with another world, mysterious and exciting, and I looked forward to those nights when, for some unknown reason, my mother pro-longed the time of prayer by singing a hymn. (She was a music teacher who had spent seven years studying in Dres-den, and had a lovely soft voice—I often reflect that the only pupils to whom she couldn't teach music were my brother and I.) The hymn I remember her singing is "There Is a Happy Land, Far, Far Away." Once again the actual meaning of the words had nothing to do with the effect of these occasions.

Let me reflect for a moment on this question of what some might call "indoctrination." If I had been composing these reflections twenty years ago—and most certainly forty years ago—I would have ripped into the theology of these Victorian children's hymns. I would have denounced—and at the time did denounce—the picture of Jesus as gentle, meek, and mild, citing his strength, his courage, and his defiance of every evil power. I would have totally rejected the notion that heaven, the eternal world, is "far, far away" and insisted that, on the contrary, it is very, very near. I would have sav-aged the hymns that said things like "Around the throne of God in heaven thousands of children stand" by remarking that they were a sad testimony to the appalling child mortality rate of Victorian days. Now I simply feel that the words didn't really matter all that much. For me they conveyed a sense of what I have to call the "holy," for there is no other word. My mother's voice singing the hymns was a real part of my "growing up with God." That's all.

I can't remember precisely when I stopped using the infant formula for prayer. There must have been one night when "Gentle Jesus" didn't come to my lips, or when my brother and I decided that we were now on our own. What remained for me was a belief that it was possible to communicate with this God who, at least sometimes, seemed to respond. The assured and totally unfanatical religion of my parents and grandparents that I have described protected me from any intolerable expectations or disappointments. God and heaven were there just as king and country were there. I was not afraid of this God, although I remember being aware that he had the advantage over any earthly powers because he was able to read my inmost thoughts and desires. Somehow God and conscience were closely intertwined. It was at this time that I conceived the idea of the Big Secret. When I lay in bed listening to the endless drone of grown-up conversation in the distance, when I caught my mother's eye meeting my father's after I had made some remark, when I watched hundreds of soldiers marching past on their way to this mystery called war, when I listened avidly for unfamiliar words in conversations (my parents had a habit of speaking in German when they didn't want us boys to understand, which accounts for my rapid acquisition of some phrases in that language and my continuing interest in foreign tongues)—at these moments I sometimes imagined that there was a big grown-up secret that I would be told when I reached a certain age. Whether I connected that secret with God I don't clearly remember, but it had to do with the mystery of a world to which I had no access at the time.

So I went on praying—not with any fixed pattern or with any unusual intensity. As I grew older I began to discover that most of my contemporaries did a bit of praying, too. There were, of course, the occasional serious conferences on such questions as the reality of fairies and Santa Claus. But I don't remember any bright boys claiming that they had discovered that God fell into the same category. I myself made a clear distinction between fairies and angels. Fairies belonged to the nursery books that we had discarded; angels were in the Bible, although I found I was not encouraged to ask too many questions about their nature and activities. Later

I had a vague impression that they were not quite accepted by Presbyterians. Of course, there was usually one boy who was rumored not to believe in God, but he was normally considered as eccentric as the passionate believer who talked about God and prayed too much. At one time the word was passed around that a bowler on the cricket team of a rival school could be seen closing his eyes in prayer before he delivered the ball, and this was considered distinctly bad form—if not seeking an unfair advantage. But I continued my fairly regular talks with God, and once experienced what I considered for years—perhaps even still consider—an extraordinary example of a directly answered prayer.

By the age of eight I had spent a peaceful year in the class of a gentle but slightly eccentric young lady (though she didn't seem very young to me then). Miss Macdonald always began the day by stopping in front of each member of the class and tapping the points of the two pencils everyone was required to have in the top breast-pocket. If the points were satisfactorily sharp, she awarded us a little piece of paper called a "Dux ticket," the purpose of which I never discovered. But the days in her classroom passed pleasantly in an atmosphere of reasonable quiet and occasional excitement—excitement which for me consisted in being thrilled by an episode of Scottish history (the books were violently nationalistic, and I reveled in the tales of William Wallace and Robert the Bruce) or being totally unable to unravel a problem in arithmetic. But Miss Macdonald was always sweet and understanding.

That was class three. But we all knew that in class four there awaited us a monster by the name of Mr. Paul. He was known to have no tolerance, either for the slightest misbehavior or for dullards in arithmetic. Since in the Junior School one was in the hands of the same teacher for the whole day, with the exception of a period spent in the gymnasium, I looked with trepidation to the coming year. In Scotland in those days, parents didn't question teachers, so there was no possibility of my parents descending on the headmaster and challenging Mr. Paul's sternness, even if I had confided my fears to them—which I hadn't.

At the beginning of the next school year I duly entered

Mr. Paul's class and found it even more unpleasant than I had expected it to be. Every night I prayed for deliverance, although I couldn't see how even God could possibly arrange it. Then after two weeks the headmaster unexpectedly entered our class. He explained that, owing to overcrowding in classes four and five, a new class called five-A was to be created; it would be made up of the top dozen of class four and the bottom dozen of class five. To my joy I qualified, and I departed in a daze of delight to the care of Miss Sandilands, thus beginning a love affair that lasted two years—in fact, a good deal longer, since I last saw her a few years ago at the age of ninety in a nursing home in Edinburgh, and had the pleasure of telling her that she was the best teacher I ever had. Her parting words to me were "Get away, flatterer!"

It may seem absurd to tell this story as a serious contribution to the literature of prayer, but I'm trying to recount what really loomed large in my childhood experience of God. There were other moments, probably much more important, when God seemed to be not just "a very present help in time of trouble" but a dimly felt yet rather exciting Presence. Such thoughts of God were related in my mind and spirit with my first realization of beauty, my enthrallment with books like *Alice in Wonderland, Treasure Island,* and tales set in earlier times and lands like ancient Egypt and Peru. It wasn't particularly in church that I had this feeling. God seemed closer to me when I was tingling with excitement about an anticipated trip to Ireland or receiving a present from my father in France or making the once-a-year visit to a theater. My parents were what you might call conscientious but not zealous church members, and during the usual Sunday morning service my attention was focused on things other than the transcendent— a funny hat on a lady in the choir, an unusually coarse word in the Scripture reading, the minister's use of his handkerchief, or the possibility of leaping from the gallery where we sat and swinging on the chandeliers until I reached the pulpit (perhaps that was a transcendent image of things to come!). But I do remember accepting worship as a reasonable way of remembering God, and on those rare occasions when I accompanied my mother to an evening service in another church,

I felt something very quiet and beautiful about the atmosphere and was very happy to be there.

I have to ask myself now if my sense of growing up with God would have been very different if my parents had been more inclined to talk about him or if my experience of prayer had been totally different. That came to mind recently when I was reading *Growing Up,* Russell Baker's delightful book about his childhood, which was completely unlike mine. What struck me was his account of his father's death when he was a small boy. When the body was brought back home, he was sent to a kindly neighbor named Bessie Scott. He writes:

> For the first time I thought seriously about God. Between sobs I told Bessie that if God could do things like this to people, then God was hateful and I had no more use for Him.
>
> Bessie told me about the peace of Heaven and the joy of being among the angels and the happiness of my father who was already there. This argument failed to quiet my rage.
>
> "God loves us all just like His own children," Bessie said.
>
> "If God loves me, why did He make my father die?"
>
> Bessie said I would understand someday, but she was only partly right. That afternoon, though I couldn't have phrased it this way then, I decided that God was a lot less interested in people than anybody in Morrisonville was willing to admit. That day I decided that God was not entirely to be trusted.
>
> After that I never cried again with any real conviction, nor expected much of anyone's God except indifference, nor loved deeply without fear that it would cost me dearly in pain. At the age of five I had become a skeptic and began to sense that any happiness that came my way might be the prelude to some grim cosmic joke.

Strangely, when I read Baker's book I did not have the impression that I was listening to a total skeptic. His recounting is infused with too much humor, too much sensitivity and hope for me to think so. But this passage depicts very movingly the crushing of a five-year-old's naive trust in God. Must we say that such an experience means growing up without God? I don't think so—any more than God had really given me up when, much later, I knew what it is to want to curse him. I don't know what my tale would be like if a telegram had come when I was five, and my mother had explained to me that my father was never coming back from France. The odds that it would happen had been about fifty-fifty; in fact, two of my father's brothers and one of my mother's dearest cousins were killed in action. I remember the sense of shock. I remember tears—but not my own. It was all rather distant, part of the grim background of war that I had come to accept as normal in those years of awakening thought from four to six. I was aware of friends who had lost their fathers, but I don't remember finding them different from the rest of us in their religion or anything else.

It seems to me now that growing up with God in my pre-adolescent years was not so much a matter of vivid experiences of a divine Person intervening in my life as of the acceptance of a divine dimension that was always there and sometimes seemed especially close. I never experienced anything comparable to a classic childhood "conversion," and when I first came in contact with anyone or anything that seemed intent on child evangelism—teachers who seemed to be pressing me to make some kind of religious decision, books that drew pictures of black hearts that had to be made snow-white, occasional evangelists who visited our school who both fascinated and disturbed me (one of them was Eric Liddell, the runner so superbly portrayed by Ian Charleson in *Chariots of Fire*), or anyone who suggested that I needed to be "saved"—I was both puzzled and repelled. I suppose my attitude was like that of the old gentleman on his deathbed who, when asked if he had made his peace with God, replied, "I didn't know there had been any rift between us." My father and mother, for different reasons, seemed to agree that this kind of religion was undesirable, and they were uncomfortable when later, for a period, I fell under its spell. What I am describing now is not an experience of growing up with God that I commend as ideal. In this book I am not in the business of commending; I am simply trying to remember and describe. And what comes back to me is a childhood religion without any stormy crises or a passionate love-hate relationship with God, but with a strong sense of what Rudolf Otto called the "numinous"—the divine dimension, the atmosphere of the holy.

Holiness in this sense attached itself to certain objects and experiences during this period of my life. There were those moments of wondering while lying flat on my back and looking up into the sky; gazing through a window at the stars; thinking about birth and death; catching the tone of voice in which my parents spoke about certain things that clearly had to do with God, though they might not mention him; being moved by a hymn or, more often and more passionately, by a pipe band (still the most emotional musical experience for me). The holy was there when one of those telegrams arrived from the front as well as when I felt intensely indignant about some story of injustice or was moved to tears by the sight of suffering. It was attached, of course, to certain objects—like those toys of my long-dead cousin, and especially to a Bible of my mother's that had belonged to one of her sisters, a singer who had died tragically at the height of her powers. That little black Bible, which was of the most unreadable variety, always represented something numinous to me, as did other mementos of the past and the war memorials that were being constructed in every town and village. A vast service, held in St. Giles in Edinburgh after the Peace of 1919, echoed in my mind for years with the words and tune of "O Valiant Hearts," which I have now forgotten.

The mention of Bibles raises the question of the part played by scriptural stories and sayings at this time in my life. I had no special Bible to which I was devoted then, although a little army edition of the New Testament that my father had given me before he left for the front in 1915 always seemed especially holy. I loved hearing tales about Samuel, David, Saul, Daniel, and other Old Testament characters, but I don't remember Jesus in particular coming to life for me in the pages of the Bible. I was comfortable with Jesus. He was most certainly a numinous figure, and I don't remember having any difficulty relating him with God. The two seemed to me to get along together—and Christological problems lay far ahead. The content of the Bible was supposed to be imparted to me at a certain hour each week in school. However little I absorbed, I do remember delighting in the rumblings of the King James' version and, on occasion, in learning passages by heart. In the same way I tolerated our headmaster's practice (he was atypically a High Anglican) of intoning prayers at chapel because I was taken by the magic of the words. (My first experience of Anglican worship was during the time my father was stationed on leave at Ripon in Yorkshire. My brother and I came home astounded at the strange ways of the English at worship, and I slightly shocked my mother by doing an imitation of the collects and responses in what you might call a "High Episcopal" voice.)

In all this you may have been looking for some early signs of a call to the ministry. To the best of my recollection there were none. Ministers were friendly but very distant figures. I was going to say "holy," but there was nothing of the numinous about the jovial figure I already described toasting my grandfather at Blacketyside. There were no clerical figures among my immediate relations, either in Scotland or in England, and it never occurred to me that there could be—although the portrait of the Reverend Samuel Martin hung in splendor in my grandfather's house. Since I now have the picture, I often look at him with affection, although he flourished long before I was born. There is that sense of assurance of his position with God and man that I have described as typical of the Church of Scotland at that time, a noble brow that seems to conceal a considerable intellect, kindly eyes that might just twinkle occasionally, and a distinct air of authority. I cannot say that as a little boy I stood and gazed on him with awe. His was just one of the pictures on the wall, vaguely connected in my mind with a much more exciting lithograph of Noah celebrating a stupendous sacrifice of thanksgiving as he emerged from the ark. Samuel Martin's chief claim to fame in Scotland is that he was the father of David Martin, a painter of distinction. So the old man (was he as old as I am now?) who might have hoped for a son to follow in his footsteps must have had at least a tolerance for the arts which, mistakenly, is not normally attributed to our Calvinist forebears.

It was much later that my father disclosed to me that there were indeed clergymen on his side of the family. I think he kept quiet about them because one was an uncle of his (younger than he was), a Methodist minister and theologian whom he could not tolerate at all, and the other was a much older uncle on his father's side who ended his days as a Church of England rector and who, not being a teetotaler like the Methodist uncle, was addicted to the bottle. In matters of drinking my father strongly disliked both extremes.

In one of Christopher Morley's novels, a girl remarks, "Pop used to say about Presbyterians, it don't prevent them committing all the sins there are, but it keeps them from getting any fun out of it." Well, that was not my experience of growing up with God, mostly among Presbyterians. I never heard those sermons about sin and damnation that so many autobiographers revel in. And however dull some religious observances seemed to me as I spent these formative years on my grandfathers' farms in Fife and in Donegal, as my brother and I came under the spell of aunts of different religious persuasions, as we settled into a school in Edinburgh when the war was over, I remember that we had a great deal of fun. And I remember many intriguing conversations that I listened to avidly. In those days, God, sex, and politics were not supposed to be discussed at the dinner table. As I remember it, God and sex certainly were not, but political talk buzzed around the table—except when that formidable liberal, my uncle Bob, came to visit Blacketyside. Yet in all this talk and activity, in all the shadows of war and the confusion of changing schools and homes, I never felt that God was out of the picture. I was even permitted to laugh a little at religion, and I had the impression that one could even laugh at death. So I was not surprised to hear, years later, that my father had done just that during the war. It was at his funeral that I was told the story—by an old man who had been a sergeant in his company. My father's Black Watch battalion had neared the front lines for the first time. The men were waiting nervously in the shelter of a village when a salvo of shells hit and totally destroyed all the houses opposite where they were stationed. "What are you worrying about?" asked my father. "You're safe as houses."

Chapter Three

PEOPLE
FLOWING
IN

In those days we weren't known as teenagers, but in due course I became one. For me it was as confusing and contradictory a period as it is now for today's generation, the only difference being that we were not segregated as a race apart and made self-conscious about our status. No one wrote books about us, nor were we subjected to interviews by the media or analyses by experts on juvenile disorders.

It is a time when most of us emerge from the family cocoon and begin to find our own way in the world. For boys like me, this meant realizing that there were other ways of living besides the way we lived at home, and many other opinions to be heard besides those of my father and mother. I went through that disturbing changeover when, after years of accepting a father's views on almost everything as inevitably correct, one begins to suspect and then finally becomes sure that these views are nearly always wrong. At this stage adolescents think that they are asserting their right to be themselves, while their parents are usually convinced that they are falling under the influence of other people. Both are right. I do remember resenting any suggestion that I was in any sense doomed to reflect my parents' likes and dislikes, prejudices, experiences, or religion. But there is no doubt whatever that I was immensely influenced by friends, teachers, older people whom I admired, and writers of all kinds who opened up new horizons for me. These were the "people flowing in" who to me were fascinating, liberating, and stimulating, but to my parents were responsible for—in their words—"putting ideas into the boy's head," not all of which were desirable.

"Flowing in" is, of course, the literal meaning of the word "influence." It's happening to all of us all of the time, no matter how assured we may be that we are immune and self-sufficient. I find it extremely difficult to sort out these influences on me during this period and, in particular, to trace their effect on that mystery that could be described as the "flowing in" of God. There was a hymn I frequently heard in church—it must have been a favorite of my minister—that had an unusually dreary tune, and for a long time it symbolized for me what seemed a particularly boring subject—the nature and work of the Holy Spirit:

> He came sweet influence to impart,
> A gracious, willing guest,
> Where he can find one humble heart
> Wherein to rest.

Influence seems to me now a perfectly good description of the Holy Spirit as God's nearness, inwardness, and guidance—indeed, exactly what I am trying to discover as God's "flowing in" at various periods of my life. Yet I still resist the picture conjured up by that hymn because it is so unlike the stimulating, tumultuous, noisy, even uproarious acts of the Holy Spirit described in the New Testament. As a boy the last thing I wanted was for anyone to try to impart "sweet influence," and I was not interested in any "gracious, willing guest" trying to come in by the back door. It was at this point that the Church began to recede from the real life I was trying to discover and became a traditional shadow hovering somewhere in the background, associated in my mind with my religious aunts and respected by my parents. In those days we had not discovered that tiresome word "relevant," but that is what the Church, for me, was not.

There may be some who grow up happily, without ever experiencing this religious revolt. However, for me at this point it was not a rejection of God but rather a total lack of interest in the institution with which he had gotten himself entangled. For a while I tolerated church services but looked forward to those occasions when there was some valid excuse (and my parents were fairly tolerant of excuses) not to go. Few of my contemporaries were what you might call church enthusiasts or devout students of the Bible. I remember how we used to envy the lone Roman Catholic in our class who was permitted to sit apart and do what he liked during the weekly period devoted to Scripture. But I mustn't overstress the "revolt" of this period. None of us complained about the restrictions that the Church had succeeded in imposing on the nation at large—no football or cricket, no movies or plays on Sunday. Nor did we feel in any way oppressed by the traditions of school prayers, grace at meals, or the occasional solemnity of the minister's pastoral visit to our homes. (I remember the warning sometimes issued at breakfast: "Be sure to be home by four. The minister is coming to tea." Believe it or not, he always appeared on these occasions, complete with frock coat and tall hat, a figure awe-inspiring yet human, with an unexpected capacity for laughter and a genuine interest in my affairs.)

Some of you may wonder why the question of confirmation did not arise at this point, forcing me to think through what I really believed and what my attitude toward the Church really was. The answer is that in the Church of Scotland, a young person was not confirmed until the age of seventeen or eighteen. To this day I don't know whether it is better to confront baptized children with this decision at about the age of thirteen on the somewhat shaky theory that "if we don't do it then, we'll lose them," or to wait for the time when they will be able to make a more mature judgment and will be less likely to associate confirmation with what Paul calls the "childhood things" they have "put away." Anyway, whatever God's dealings with me were at this time, they seem to have included letting me run pretty loose from his Church.

It's hard for me to define how school influenced me at

this age. Among my memories is the awesome figure of our headmaster, who once presented me unexpectedly with a Greek New Testament, just after I had been given the option of renouncing such science as was offered and beginning the study of Greek. My scientific education thus came to an abrupt halt when I was thirteen, not because I had any desire to be able to read the New Testament in its original tongue but because I was delighted to exchange a subject that involved figures, which I hated, for one that involved words, which I loved. Once a week visiting ministers used to teach Bible in every class. They ranged from earnest evangelicals to young men who tried to shock us with advanced theories of biblical criticism. We accepted them all with equal indifference. The only one who enchanted us was an ex-serviceman who not only was a superb soccer player but had a unique gift for launching a piece of chalk in the direction of the inattentive and hitting them with remarkable accuracy. (He subsequently became Moderator of the General Assembly.) On a different level of Bible study, I remember being met in the cloakroom one morning by an excited little friend who produced a Bible and showed me a verse in Isaiah that contained at least two naughty and forbidden words.

During this time I was enormously influenced by teachers who introduced me to the world of literature—English, French, Latin, and Greek. I reveled in Shakespeare and Milton, was intoxicated by the lyrics of Keats and Shelley, and voluntarily memorized screeds of Scottish ballads and Macaulay's *Lays of Ancient Rome*. On the stage I threw myself into every part that came my way, ending, I hoped triumphantly, by portraying Brutus in *Julius Caesar* and Malvolio in *Twelfth Night*. We had a French teacher, Monsieur Meslier, who was so thoroughly French that he allowed no English to be spoken in his classroom. To him I owe some of my first trips abroad, because at Eastertime he used to take about forty of us to France, where we stayed at school and explored the city or the countryside. My eyes were being opened to other ways of eating and drinking, other ways of thinking about what was right or wrong, all of it with a totally different religious backdrop. Monsieur Meslier was a devout Roman Catholic, and I remember standing with him in the cathedral of Beauvais while he explained to me how those majestic pillars led one's thoughts up to God—a new idea for me, who until then had found little in the churches I knew to suggest any such thing.

One of the strongest influences on me was our chief English teacher, a gentle but determined scholar known affectionately as "Sluggy," who found me an unusually receptive listener to his readings from the poets and an eager participant who was always ready to argue about their respective merits. I mention him particularly because for years I often visited his home and even inflicted on him my first efforts at verse. Like most of the lyrical efforts of people my age, my poems tended to be somewhat tragic in tone and full of Keatsian yearnings. From my recollections of his kindly comments, I later realized that he was suggesting that my poetic talents were better suited to light verse and the limerick. But religion was often the subject of our talks. He was a believer—even that rare phenomenon, a Scottish Baptist—but he was anxious to protect me from falling prey to what he called Govan's "fundamentalism," a word that was new to me.

Govan's name leads me to the influence of my friends and contemporaries. Govan was one of several boys who were close friends of mine, and he was notorious for his intense religious convictions. What first drew me to him, however, was not his passion for the Christian gospel so much as his enthusiasm for locomotives and his ability, which I totally lacked, to draw them to perfection. (One of my first published works was in a class magazine in which I expatiated on the different types of engines to be seen in Scotland, an article for which Govan provided superb illustrations.) I also admired his determination, his ability to transcend average schoolboy morals without appearing too much of a prig, and his fondness for debating, which I shared. (In Scottish schools and universities there is ample opportunity to learn to discourse without notes on almost any subject and to find arguments in support of almost any cause. I was thrown in at the deep end at the age of twelve.)

My closest friend, however, was one James Cowie, who was almost completely different from me in physical build, scholastic preferences, and temperament. That meant that we came at most subjects from totally different directions and that we argued long into the night; we also enjoyed each other's company, and later explored foreign countries together. Cowie, whose father was a dealer in antiques, came flowing into my life with a knowledge of art, a skill in science, and a surprisingly mature judgment of people, politics, and religion. I loved to listen to his father as he sucked on his clay pipe and shared his vigorous opinions on everybody from Mr. Ramsay MacDonald, whom he detested, to his local minister, whom he despised. Although he was by no means a skeptic, he had a lack of enthusiasm for the Church that dated from the time his minister arrived on his doorstep, saying, "I'm afraid I can only spare you half an hour, Mr. Cowie," to which he replied, "I'm afraid I can't spare you even that," and shut the door.

I am tempted to speak of other boys who flowed into my life in these early days. One was Eric Ghosh, the son of an Indian father and a Scottish mother, who was my closest friend for the two years we were together until he mysteriously disappeared with his father to India. And there was a host of others, from Alex Munro, who combined brilliance in almost every subject with precocious skill in cricket and rugby, to the boy who rejoiced in the name of Milton but who inevitably finished at the bottom of the class in our literary examinations—thereby drawing sad and supposedly witty comment from our scholarly head. But I must get back to the religious area, where Govan was the moving spirit.

For a few years Govan made repeated attempts to get me to attend evangelistic meetings designed for schoolboys. There was usually the promise of free tea and cream buns, so quite a number of us attended them from time to time. We would find ourselves in what was, by our standards, a rather grand drawing room. After downing the refreshments, we were directed to a row of chairs, on each of which lay a hymnbook. I remember distinctly the shock this gave me the first time. Hymnbooks, in my sense of fitness, belonged to Sunday only—and this was a Saturday evening. The highlight of these occasions was always a talk in which the speaker seemed to assume that, with the exception of one or two, we all stood in urgent need of conversion to Christ. I confess that some of these talks moved me, but they also made me extremely uncomfortable. I was made aware that this religious business was much more important than I had imagined, but I couldn't quite see why I should seek this conversion experience when I wasn't honestly conscious of being in any way opposed to this Christ whom I was invited to receive for the first time. In addition, I was both fascinated and repelled by the fact that nearly all the speakers at these meetings were afflicted with some kind of facial tic—a popping of the eyebrows or a twist of the mouth. I also remember picking up a little tract in which it was suggested that, once one became a Christian, certain activities were taboo—particularly smoking, drinking, dancing, and going to the movies and the theater. It was this last that outraged me, and I glanced at the arguments that were offered. "At your age," I read (I remember the phrasing), "you cannot possibly know of the years of sin and degradation connected with the stage." I turned to my friend Cowie and confided in a whisper that I thought I knew a great deal more about the stage than the writer of the booklet. I allowed Govan to haul me to a number of these meetings, including one in a big hall where a celebrated evangelist delivered a highly emotional address. I think it was on this occasion that I was later interrogated by my mother, who was a little anxious about the effect such meetings had on me.

"Did he smile a lot?" she asked.

"Yes," I replied. "They always do." That set me thinking.

These attempts to convert me had the opposite effect: I not only avoided this kind of religion for some years but gradually began to delight in people and books that attacked conventional Christianity in all its forms—provided the attack was waged with logic and wit. Among others, George Bernard Shaw came flowing in. I devoured the prefaces of his plays, in which he challenged all the accepted religious and ethical judgments of our time, and reveled in his demolition of what he called "Crosstianity." I went to as many of his plays as I could when a repertory company came to Edinburgh; a seat in the gallery cost sixpence. This company actually produced *Man and Superman* in its entirety—including the hell scene—

a feat that lasted six hours. I went every night of that week at a cost of a penny an hour, and then had the supreme joy of being invited by a friend, whose father was an actor, to do a walk-on part of about three words. (This was a time when I seriously considered becoming an actor, although a subsequent evening spent in the dingy lodging house of a bit-part actor whom I met in a Shakespeare company disillusioned me about the glamour of the profession.)

H. G. Wells was another discovery I made at this time. I remember being impressed by his debunking of the importance of Bible history, and by his dismissal of all that the churches had to say about sin and depravity. His *Outline of History* ends with a glowing account of humanity on the march into a "brave new world." (His last book, *Mind at the End of Its Tether*, which appeared at the end of World War II, offered a very different picture—but that was beyond my horizon when I was a teenager.) "Brave new world" was, of course, the phrase not of Wells but of Aldous Huxley, writing in the period of disillusionment. And Huxley, in his earlier days, soon became one of my intellectual heroes. His clarity, his wit, his way of needling all the people whose morality I was supposed to respect proved a great attraction to me as my school days neared an end. Another good friend, whose father—a minister—had bestowed on him the name of Archibald Hamilton Charteris Phinn Gillison and who later became one of the early atomic scientists, was always a good source of inside information about the follies of fundamentalism, and my discussions with Govan once again focused on railways and locomotives.

When I recall that during these years I experienced the loss of a classmate who died of meningitis, and that two years later my life hung by a thread after an attack of acute peritonitis, it seems odd that I have little recollection of doing any serious thinking about God or the afterlife during this period. I don't remember doing any praying, and although a religious aunt gave me what was called a "Bible for Youth," which I found mildly interesting, I certainly never leaned on the Bible for daily support. If I was an agnostic, I didn't particularly want to advertise the fact. My parents, of course, would never have understood, and I had no desire to rock the steady boat of conventional religion. If you had asked me at this point what I wanted to do with my life, I would have replied without hesitation that I wanted to get the best possible degree in English literature at the university, and would have mentioned with considerable hesitation that thereafter I might teach, enter the diplomatic or consular service, or become an advocate (the Scottish equivalent of the English barrister—the one who does the pleading in court) or a journalist. If anyone had mentioned the ministry, I would have smiled and changed the subject. It never even crossed my mind. I had nothing against ministers, but so far I had never heard a sermon that aroused in me more than a desire to argue.

"But God . . . ," as the Bible often says. What are these strange twists and turns that lead us to new convictions and in new directions? When I speak of the "hand of God," I don't imply that he deliberately mapped out for me every succeeding chapter in my life and necessarily intended me to go through each experience and succumb to each new influence. I may be happy to be called a Calvinist, but not too happy if that word implies that I really had no choice or that every influence upon me was necessarily the will of God. Surely all of us can think of directions we shouldn't have taken and influences we would have been much better off without. But I grow more and more convinced of the truth of Paul's conviction that God "works for good *in all things*"—in other words, that whatever follies or misfortunes we can trace in our past, we can also trace ways in which God brought us through them. We can't rejoice in the follies or misfortunes that may have warped us in some way or hurt other people, but we can see how God worked in everything and we can, by his grace, rise above the level of our regrets. But before I begin to preach, let me return to my adolescent flirtation with agnosticism and the upheaval that followed it.

Govan never gave up. Eventually he persuaded me to attend a summer camp run by a group of undergraduates and a few older people—lawyers, doctors, and an occasional young clergyman. My friend Cowie assured me that I would enjoy it, so I signed up for one of the two weeks, reckoning that the fun would be worth any overdose of religion. That something happened to me at this camp the first time I attended it is clear from the fact that I went back again and again for twelve years. What I experienced was a splendid holiday in magnificent surroundings in the Highlands, with games, expeditions, concerts, and songs, and the companionship of about a hundred boys roughly my own age. Through it all came a strong religious pressure that I partly resisted and partly accepted with joy. The resistance I have already explained. But what brought about this new acceptance of a distinctly fundamentalist exposition of the gospel? I can think of at least three factors. First, the people I met there were by no means products of the same conventional evangelical mold. They shared a common social background, but their interests and abilities varied. They didn't have facial tics. They seemed to enjoy life to the full. And they were able to laugh—even at some of their own peculiar religious practices. Second, having just come from a cadet corps military camp, I found the atmosphere here very different. Segregate boys (or anyone else, as I was to learn later) in the confines of a camp, and a climate develops that either raises or lowers the moral temperature of each individual. That's what I think Reinhold Niebuhr is saying in his *Moral Man and Immoral Society*. What I was really saying to myself, then, was something like, "They've got some funny ideas, but if this is the Christian life, I'm all for it." Third, for the first time that I could remember I was hearing about Christ as a real person whom I could get to know. Sitting with others in a lamp-lit tent at night or going off alone for a while into the mountains, I had a clear sense of the living presence of Christ—something beyond the historical character whom I had professed to admire while I rejected orthodox beliefs about him.

I did *not* undergo any catastrophic conversion. In fact, I discovered that, although the talks morning and evening kept stressing the need for such an experience, the speakers I talked to nearly always confessed that they themselves couldn't name the day and the hour that they had become believers. "You see," each used to add apologetically, "I was raised in a Christian home"—leaving me wondering if I hadn't been. I left that camp with a great love for the gospel that was being proclaimed and lived, an admiration for the powerful and biblical talks of the camp leader, and a feeling of having been brought under the spell of a living Lord. For that I must, and do, remain grateful.

Having said this, I can now list all that was wrong with these camps that I continued to attend for so many years. There was far too much pressure put on boys to make a decision that many I knew subsequently rejected. There was too much jargon about "quiet times," "coming through," how not to be "worldly" (I noticed that it was "worldly" to smoke or dance but not to spend lavish sums on sports cars and fancy clothes). There was an unspoken but subtle tendency to equate sin with the sexual instincts of growing boys. And there was nothing said about our Christian responsibility for the less privileged around us and the issues of war and peace—it is hard now to believe that I am talking about a period when the Depression had forced millions to depend on what we called "the dole," and when Hitler was already casting his shadow over Europe.

Well, there I was on my way to becoming, if not a dyed-in-the-wool fundamentalist, at least a fervid evangelical ready to do battle for the faith and, for a time at least, abiding by most of the prohibitions that ran quite counter to my inclinations. My God, as it were, had become much more real and vital, but he was now somewhat narrow-minded. And, as John Donne wisely wrote, "Never propose to thyself such a God as thou art not bound to imitate." With enthusiasm I plunged back into my studies and hobbies and pursued my ambitions. Strangely enough, my newfound faith never suggested for a moment that I should become a minister. I had succumbed to one of the defects of this movement—a tendency to think of most churches as dead and their clergy as, at best, backsliders. Thus, during a period when it is natural to have strong and somewhat intolerant views, I was emerging as an enthusiastic member of an evangelical movement that crossed denominational lines and stood outside the historic community I now recognize as the Holy Catholic Church.

My parents must have found me difficult to cope with in

this ultra-evangelical phase, but preferred it to my becoming a fascist or a communist, a Roman Catholic or a libertine. My father, whose idea of churchmanship was "Low prayer-book Anglican," was satisfied with the theology I had embraced, although I remember his commenting negatively on the Scofield edition of the King James' Bible I proudly showed him: it had omitted the splendid dedication to "the most high and mighty Prince James, by the grace of God, King of Great Britain, France and Ireland." He was relieved that my new religious friends showed little inclination to the pacifism that was rampant at the time. My mother, while I think she regretted my becoming one of those whom she had been trained to recognize as "pi" (a goody-goody), may have secretly nourished the hope that it might all be resolved by my becoming a minister. But much was to happen before that call came hurtling in my direction.

Chapter Four

THEOLOGY
AT
WORK

Looking back, I think it would have been better for me, on leaving school, to go to a university outside of Edinburgh. It's always good for a student to spend his university days in a new environment, but for me, in particular, it would have been an emancipation to be cut loose from the constraints, not just of family but of the network of associations I had formed—the "old school ties," the specific religious commitments, the stifling effect of what Glasgow people recognize as Edinburgh stuffiness. But that experience was to come later, after my graduation, when I spent a year in France. In the meantime, financial considerations precluded any ideas of attending Oxford or Cambridge, and local prejudice ruled out the only rival Scottish universities—St. Andrew's, Glasgow, and Aberdeen. Edinburgh might be the "newcomer," having been founded in 1583, but to us there was no question about its superiority, especially in the arts and in medicine (my brother had already entered that department). And how could any serious student pass up the opportunity to study English literature under the great Herbert Grierson, the man who had put John Donne back on the literary map, or the chance to study Greek under the eccentric, lovable, and fantastically erudite Alexander Mair?

So it was to Edinburgh University that I took my scholarly ambitions, my fervid evangelicism, my growing curiosity, and my innocence. These were all strangely mixed up in the undergraduate years that followed. I was still trailing the clouds of a religious ardor that was nourished by the Bible camps I attended and by new associations with like-minded evangelicals. At the same time I had scholastic ambitions, and so certain tensions inevitably developed.

There was, for one thing, the allocation of time. I had assumed responsibility for a weekly Bible class in an organization known as the Crusaders; I was active in the student group connected with the IVF (the Inter-Varsity Fellowship, which is still very much alive); I was involved in the Scripture Union, which encouraged Bible-reading among schoolchildren; and I read the Bible regularly, in addition to reading a lot of books that advocated the religious party-line that I still adhered to. This meant that a great deal of my spare time was spent on other things than my set studies. And it meant that my time on weekends, when my fellow students were mostly absorbed in Beowulf, Chaucer, Shakespeare, and such, was totally swallowed up. I spent most of Saturday at the sports field of my own school, refereeing rugby games in the morning and playing in the afternoon. (I should note here that, having been unable to participate in games at school after an operation, I was making up for it in a big way. I was a very mediocre performer on the rugby field but enjoyed the game enormously. It had something to do with my newfound zeal for the Christian ideal of the total fitness of mind, body, and soul. It was also a good release for passionate emotions. Not even a great evangelistic meeting with the most stirring speaker could arouse in me such wild and vociferous enthusiasm as, for instance, the annual rugby international, in which England was the antagonist.) Sunday, according to my strict convictions, was reserved for religion. Work of any kind was out of the question, and so were games. I had no difficulty in identifying with our Olympic hero, Eric Liddell, and his famous refusal to run on Sundays.

On the other hand, the honors course in what was called "Rhetoric and English Literature" offered an intellectual challenge, I was just beginning to realize. Perhaps to discourage many of us who thought it would be delightful to while away the university years with a leisurely perusal of our favorite poets, the authorities threw in our path two intensive years of philology. We were required to learn not only Anglo-Saxon but every dialect thereof, as well as some Icelandic. We were also required to know the intricate dialects of Middle English and Middle Scots; we had to recognize each on sight and be able to comment accurately on the differences between them. This was not at all what I had had in mind when I had anticipated frolicking in the fields of literature. Worse still, one was required to pass an exam at the end of these two years, and failure meant exclusion from the final honors exam in literature. The capping disillusionment was my discovery that a failure to reach a certain level very early on meant the same fate. I got my first shock when, after an early exam, the lecturer announced that those who had failed to reach a mark of forty percent could give up any idea of an honors degree. I darted off to retrieve my papers and with a wildly beating heart saw inscribed on the front page "41%." I took that quite seriously as a message from God and began to reconsider my priorities. Two years later, when the dreaded final honors exam was looming, I remember saying to an earnest leader of one of the evangelical groups I was working with, who was pressing me to accept some new responsibility with the implication that it was God's will, "Don't you think it might be God's will for me to get a first-class honors degree?"

I leave it to you to decide whether God was nudging me in that direction, and whether he was indeed much concerned with my academic record. I know that I learned then—just in the nick of time—that in the matter of exam results, prayer is no substitute for hard work. It was dawning on me that my Christian discipleship meant something more inclusive than membership in a coterie of the devout and attempts to draw others into the same fold. Still with no specific career goal in view, I began to sense the breadth of the kingdom of God and the narrowness of the boundaries in which I had set it. I made some adjustments in my timetable, and although I never attained a first-class certificate in any one term, the overall results were good: to the surprise of most of my friends (and, I suspect, my teachers), I emerged from the final exams with the coveted *summa cum laude.* I think my attitude then was "This is the Lord's doing and wonderful in my eyes."

All this time another tension was mounting. I had come to a very real and compelling belief in Christ within the fold of an evangelical movement that held to a rigid theological position and a fairly clearly defined stance on what activities were legitimate for the genuine Christian. The theological dogma and the moral implications were mirrored in the peculiar jargon we used within those circles. We judged speakers at meetings and preachers in churches to be "sound" or "unsound." If the word went around that a certain speaker was voicing opinions contrary to the strict orthodoxy we believed—suggesting, for instance, that there might be more than one way of interpreting the Cross of Christ, or that within the Bible there were divergent theological perspectives, or that the Bible might not be entirely inerrant on matters of history or geology or astronomy—we wrote him off as "unsound." Another weighted word was "keen." If one of our number strayed from the accepted behavior, perhaps known to indulge in an occasional cigarette or seen coming out of a movie theater, it was soon common knowledge that he or she was no longer "keen." The "unkeen" were regarded as second-class Christians and would certainly not be invited to lead any Bible class or discussion group.

As you can imagine, this combination of rigid dogma and narrow definition of the Christian life bothered me more and more as I launched into the strange new world of academic mind-stretching. Increasingly I felt the tug of much of the fun I seemed to be missing unnecessarily. I don't want to leave the impression that my so-called Christian witness excluded me entirely from the natural exuberance of student life. When we ran loose among the sober Edinburgh citizens during the annual Charity Week, for instance, I reveled in contributing to our spoof newspapers, and once spent a riotous morning as an amateur traffic-cop in Princes Street. I didn't take the debates of the Dialectical Society, a venerable institution dating back to the early eighteenth century, with grim seriousness, and I thoroughly enjoyed exchanging witticisms with atheists, socialists, and sticklers for the time-honored rules by which we were bound. I loved crossing swords verbally with contemporaries who, as I remember, later became professors of philosophy, notorious advocates of what was then known as "free love," moderators of the Kirk, and even cabinet ministers. All this was immensely stimulating, but in the wings I always heard the warning voice of those who spoke about "worldly amusements" and the necessity of remaining uncorrupted by false doctrine or the enticements of ways of thought that were summed up by the sinister word "modernism."

If it seems odd that, with my growing intellectual curiosity and my natural propensity for the lighter side of university life, I should have remained attached to this rigid theology and narrow interpretation of the Christian life, the answer must be found in my conviction that, if I wandered from the environment in which I had found the living Christ, I should soon find myself back in the dreary and timid agnosticism from which I had been delivered. At the time there seemed to be no middle choice between a kind of fundamentalism that troubled the mind and paralyzed the spirit but boldly proclaimed Jesus Christ, crucified and risen from the dead as the one Lord and Savior, and a theological liberalism that seemed to me then little more than agnosticism with a halo. The answer to this dilemma was soon to come, but during this interim period the choice seemed to be between a belief in a living Christ with lots of uncomfortable strings attached and a plunge into the murky waters where one was no longer "sound" and most definitely not "keen."

It was during this tense period that something happened that I don't think I have ever before set down in writing, and have confessed only to a very few. I remember clearly that one evening I was obsessed by questions about what career I should choose. Teaching? Yes; I saw the attraction of a life devoted to awakening the love of literature in others, and perhaps steering them gently toward a Christian faith. Diplomacy? Yes; I would enjoy representing my country in international politics and fulfilling a Christian ambition to work for peace and understanding. The bar? Yes; I could see myself defending a just cause with all the eloquence I could summon. Journalism? Yes; I could imagine the excitement of being on the scene when great things happened and phrasing my accounts of them so as to suggest a Christian meaning. But which was the will of God for me? I knelt for a time in prayer. As I rose to my feet, a crazy idea gripped me and made me do something I not only despised but had frequently warned the boys in my Bible class never to do. I opened my Bible at random, shut my eyes, and plunged my finger on a verse. What I read was "Go thou and preach the Kingdom of God." Am I confessing that this was my call to the Christian ministry, that I accepted this sign as a clear answer to my prayers? On the contrary, I was horrified at what I had done. It was superstition; it was almost blasphemy. I was so ashamed that I thrust the words aside and for at least a year afterward never let my mind even drift toward the idea of becoming a preacher. What was happening in that mysterious terrain of the unconscious I leave to the psychiatrists.

I dived back into my books with enthusiasm, stimulated not only by my teachers but by a variety of entertaining friends who loved to argue. Three in particular attracted me. There was Robert Dunnett, the son of my minister—for whom I had great respect, though I wondered occasionally if he was really "sound"—who went into journalism and later became a well-known war correspondent for the BBC. We used to walk home from classes together, discussing not only the books we were reading but religion, politics, rugby football, and the local clergy. He was a model of politeness, so he seldom challenged any of my more outrageous views, but he opened my eyes to the possibility that there was a world of culture from which a Christian need not, *ipso facto*, be excluded. There was David Rintoul, who was somewhat older than the rest of us because he had spent some years working in a paper mill, and whose contribution to our discussions was a refreshing breeze from a very different world. He was one of the most honest and direct men I have ever known. No flimsy sense of manners ever inhibited him from telling us exactly what he thought, and what he had to say was usually salutary. "The trouble with you, Read," he announced one day, after I had been waxing lyrical over one of Donne's sonnets, "is that you're not a critic; you're an enthusiast." To this day his yearly letter to me brings back these rhythms of speech in which he delivered shrewd comments on everything and everyone with fear or favor. He has spent most of his professional life as an inspiring teacher in my old school. And then there was Hector McIver, a Highlander. He brought to us his soft Celtic voice, his mystic vision, and his entrancing stories about ghosts, second sight, and Gaelic lore. He was a superb raconteur, and years later, when he dropped in on our manse in Edinburgh after spending some time as an able seaman in the Royal Navy during the war, he held us spellbound with such tales. In our student days he helped to open my reluctant eyes to the Celtic element in our literary heritage. I had always favored the Lowlands, and one of the first pieces I succeeded in selling to a local paper had been a loaded argument based on the fact that the best-known Scottish writers—Walter Scott, Robert Burns, Robert Louis Stevenson, and the like—were all Lowlanders. But Hector broke down this bias of mine and introduced me to the Highland world. He became a well-known figure in Scottish literary circles and was a beloved teacher at the Royal High School until his untimely death.

In the Honors School each of us was allotted a special period of English literature for intensive study—either the sixteenth, the seventeenth, or the eighteenth century. I had hoped for the seventeenth so that I might revel in the metaphysical poets with Grierson. I would have tolerated the nineteenth, since Keats, Shelley, Byron, and even Wordsworth still appealed to the Romantic in me. But I drew the eighteenth, thereby preparing for another conversion. For in two years I lost interest in the Romantics and was captivated by Alexander Pope, came under the spell of Samuel Johnson, and delighted in the lapidary style of Swift, Addison, and Steele. The flow of rational argument, the balanced sentences, the elegance with which they used the heroic couplet, the wit, the common sense, the polished manner in which they "surveyed mankind, from China to Peru"—all this now enthralled me, and, like most converts, I looked with shame on my past infatuations and judged them all by the standards of the Augustan age. Keats and Shelley belonged to my adolescence. Wordsworth (whom my teacher at this time, himself an Augustan, used to refer to as "old W. W.") I banished from my reading until I recovered my equilibrium later on. This moving from one extreme to the other is fairly typical of the student mind, but I have been wondering recently if there was some connection between literary and theological "conversion" at this time. Surely Milton aroused tremendous echoes in me with the resounding language of *Paradise Lost* and the haunting beauty of "Lycidas," and the metaphysical poets opened my eyes to the depths of Christian devotion in souls remote from evangelical conventions. "Batter my heart, three-personed God," quoted Rintoul to me one day, and added, "Did you never feel like that?" But what did this newfound delight in the clarity, balance, and elegance of the Augustans signify in my theological development, in my Christian devotion?

It was probably a reflection of my inner desire to be rid of the emotional untidiness of the piety I had accepted, the rejection of great tracts of rich human experience, and the irrational elements in the dogma that I had swallowed whole. I was feeling my way toward a theology that didn't offend my intelligence, such as it was, toward a way of life that was free from the inhibitions of the extremely devout. I had to think through my beliefs clearly and honestly, not keep them locked up in a separate corner of my mind. And it began to dawn on me that "Thou shalt not smoke" was nowhere written in Scripture, that Christians better than I were happily free from the petty taboos that I had accepted, and that it would be much better for my soul on occasion to take a girl to the movies rather than go to a prayer meeting.

Then one day God's time bomb exploded. If the devil had also had a time bomb waiting for me, I suppose I might have suddenly thrown overboard all my religious conviction, might have reveled in scarifying my previous mentors (perhaps even writing the kind of play now common on Broadway, in which the author spills out the debris of a youthful religiosity—usually Roman Catholic), and sought some really hedonistic lifestyle. But God had other plans for me—and the most sudden, unexpected, and radical turnabout occurred about a year before I graduated.

At that time every Sunday morning found me dutifully attending church with my parents. In the afternoon I had my Bible class, and in the evening I went to listen to one of a variety of preachers—most of whom we deemed "sound" or as nearly "sound" as a Church of Scotland minister could be expected to be. Among them were James Black, James Stewart, George Macleod, and occasional English visitors like Bryan Green. My favorite was an unlikely choice. To begin with, his name was Scroggie, and he looked it. On top of that, he was a Baptist, and his church was a little chapel tucked away on Rose Street—a lane between Princes Street and George Street, ignored by visitors but frequented by the natives of the section because of its unusual variety of pubs. Scroggie had no theatrical gestures like James Black, no charisma like George Macleod, no dramatic fervor like James Stewart, and no devastating charm like Bryan Green. He simply expounded the Bible steadily and logically, not without passion but with a curious dryness that didn't seem to suit his congregation. As a well-known speaker at the Keswick Convention, he was much in demand in evangelical as well as fundamentalist circles. It was at the Keswick Convention that evangelicals from all over Britain met once a year for an orgy of preaching. There was talk about the power of the Spirit, about a "second blessing," and about victory over our besetting sins. I once heard Scroggie relate an anecdote about a lady at the convention who had asked him how to conquer her sin of lying in bed too long in the morning. His reply was "Madam, I advise you to put one foot out of bed and draw the other after it." You can see why it was not only his ability as a biblical expositor that appealed to me.

One Sunday evening I made my way to Charlotte Chapel, looking forward to hearing Scroggie—who often preached for nearly an hour. To my disappointment I found that he was somewhere else that night, but after a moment's hesitation I decided to stay where I was and take whatever came. To this day I cannot tell you what came. I remember neither the preacher's name nor anything he said. What I do remember, with luminous clarity, was that in the middle of the sermon I was suddenly and totally convinced that God wanted me to be a minister. Nothing whatever was being said on that subject, and in any case my attention had wandered. All I can say is that if any friend had asked me as I entered that church what I was going to do with my life, I would have replied with the usual list of alternatives that were still in my mind. If anyone had asked me the same question on my way out I would have replied, "Don't ask me why just now, but I know that I'm going to be ordained a minister."

No other religious experience, before or since, has ever hit me with such suddenness and force. It was an irresistible call of God, the nearest thing I have ever known to actually hearing him speak. Since then I have never had any real difficulty with the passages in the Bible where Moses or the prophets are recorded as saying, "Thus saith the Lord . . ." or "The Word of the Lord came to me, saying. . . ." I don't mean that I believed that I had joined the august company of prophets and apostles and was about to deliver the oracles of God from thenceforth. It was just that an overwhelming conviction of what to do, and perhaps what to say, had swept over me. From that moment on I had no doubt whatever that I was called to preach, and only in very dire moments when the whole structure of my faith seemed threatened did I ever even momentarily consider any other line of employment.

It would not be difficult to analyze what happened that Sunday night and demonstrate that it was the climax of a subconscious struggle, dating perhaps from my furious rejection of the Bible-dipping episode I have described. Some might note that I had been enacting my version of the classic pattern of resisting God's call. I knew I wasn't a Gideon or a Jeremiah or a Paul, but I was familiar with the accounts of their refusal to accept the message. And we all know that even the most sudden and dramatic conversions have their roots in past experiences, and although I had not experienced any such conversion to Christ, here was my call to the ministry coming in this cataclysmic way. At the time I was not at all interested in any such "explanations," and, frankly, they don't much

THEOLOGY AT WORK

interest me now. I know now, as I knew then, that the call
came—and I am grateful. The methods God uses to reveal
himself to us at turning points in our lives are not really our
business. I have friends in the ministry who are clearly fulfilling God's will for their lives who never had any such overwhelming experience. There are hundreds of pastors and
preachers better than I who could not date so precisely their
call to the ministry. What it did for me was virtually eliminate
all doubt about whether I had made the right choice. It has
also given me strong convictions about the ministry as a particular calling, the significance of ministerial ordination, and
has thus made me hostile to current trends to depreciate the
office and homogenize the Church. What we have been seeing
recently under the banner of "the priesthood of all believers"
is not so much all laypersons becoming priests as a tendency
for all priests to become laypersons.

That night I left Charlotte Chapel elated in spirit but very
confused about what my next step should be. I don't remember breaking the news to my parents that night, but I went
to bed with my mind spinning with the thrilling possibilities
that lay ahead. In the cool light of morning, common sense
took over, and it was clear that the first thing to do was to
complete my degree in literature and then decide how, where,
and when I should begin theological studies. It also seemed
a good idea to seek out some older friends in the ministry—
"sound" ones, if possible—tell them what had happened, and
ask for their advice. I regret to report that these consultations
had only one benefit: I made a resolution to the effect that
when I eventually became a minister, I would do more listening than talking when someone came to me for advice. It
seemed to me that these good men scarcely heard what I was
saying and couldn't wait to talk about their own adventures
in the ministry.

A minor crisis erupted a little later. The evangelical organizations with which I was connected employed some young
men and women in full-time jobs, and I was invited to spend
a year in such a position. I thought it would be a good idea
to take the opportunity before I entered seminary. My father
violently opposed the idea, and I see now that he was right,

although at the time the disagreement was painful. Fortunately, another proposition surfaced unexpectedly just then, and this time my views and my father's enthusiastically coincided. I learned from a friend that I could get a scholarship that would take me to France for a year to study at three Protestant seminaries in Montpellier, Strasbourg, and Paris. It carried the princely sum of a hundred pounds (five hundred dollars at the current rate of exchange). If you wonder why my father and I felt this was really a good proposition, I have to include a footnote about my enduring passion for travel (particularly at someone else's expense) and our common fondness for France and the French.

In those days it was relatively cheap to cross the Channel from any of the ports, from Southampton in the south to Leith, which was on our doorstep, and living in France or Belgium was astonishingly inexpensive. So from the age of about fourteen I traveled with my father—and sometimes my mother—and we explored such places as Bruges, Brussels, Paris, Dieppe, Rouen, and Strasbourg. When I traveled with my father, we were what are now called backpackers. We stayed in tiny railway hotels, ate in *prix fixe* restaurants, and drank coffee—and, when I was older, wine—in innumerable sidewalk cafés. My father's passion for military history took us to places like Waterloo, Sedan, and Metz, as well as some of the World War I battlefields. I confess that there were times when his enthusiasm and inexhaustible knowledge aroused in me at least some echo of the pacifism that was capturing some of my student friends then. Sometimes I wanted to interrupt and shout, "Why can't we wander through this lovely country without talking about machine guns and maneuvers and casualties?" But I was infinitely grateful for this introduction to the joys of foreign travel. I still know the thrill that comes from stepping off the boat and boarding a train that clatters its way through the port and then speeds out into the fair French countryside. And I still know the enchantment of hearing called out—when the train stops at stations in the night—the magic names of French cities: Avignon, Orange, Trascon, Arles, Marseilles.

This scholarship offered the entrancing prospect of a

Wanderjahr, as the Germans call it, combined with adventures in theology that I still approached with a certain amount of suspicion, and the opportunity—at last—to break out of the narrow circles in which I had been moving. What God had in store for me I couldn't possibly have guessed. It was to be a year I would never forget, a year I wouldn't have missed for anything—even a year in the United States.

Chapter Five

THEOLOGY
AT
WAR

In September 1932 I forwarded a big trunk to Montpellier in the south and set off for my year in France. Since the semester didn't begin until October, I had a month to fill, and I contemplated buying a motorcycle with which to explore the area. But my funds wouldn't stretch quite that far, so I settled for an ordinary bike and set off along the Riviera with a minimum of impedimenta. Since I had exactly twenty pounds saved up for this tour, every penny counted. I stayed in some fearsome hotels because my spending limit was ten francs a night (about twenty cents), and I ate more horsemeat than I ever consumed before or since. But eventually I reached Nice, where the sight of a boat leaving for Corsica evoked memories of "Colomba" and the maquis. I consulted maps, guides, and my funds, and decided that it would be better to push on into Italy and try to return another way. For those interested in my religious and literary interests at this time, I must record that besides a spare shirt, a pair of socks, and toilet articles, I carried in my knapsack a Bible and a collection of the stories of P. G. Wodehouse. Each I read every night with almost equal devotion.

I met some interesting people en route to Genoa, which seemed about as far as my budget would take me. There I found a freighter that was sailing for Barcelona, and I decided that Spain might offer me some new experiences on my way back to Montpellier. After a rough voyage over a turbulent Mediterranean, I paid out almost all of my remaining cash to the Spanish customs officials as a deposit on the importation of my bike; I was promised that it would be returned to me as I crossed the border to France. After a taste of Spanish life, including a fireworks display and a visit to an ultramodern cathedral that I thought was hideous,* I pedaled off toward the Pyrenees. As I struggled up the last few kilometers to the border, I fell in with some young Germans. Since I had not yet learned their language, we talked by making signs and mentioning place-names. I drew a large circle in the air with my finger and announced, "Montpellier, Marseilles, Nice, Genoa, Barcelona, Verona, Montpellier," but I was deflated by their response: "Munich, Rome, Naples, Morocco, Gibraltar, Barcelona, Paris, Munich." This was one of several times that I felt rather crushed by the new generation of German youth. My swing along the coast of the Mediterranean and my sampling of three countries (four, if you count Monaco, which I had sped through without noticing) had ended ingloriously within twenty miles of Montpellier. The front-brake cable on my bike had swung loose and plunged into the wheel as I was coasting at great speed down a long hill, and I had limped back to my lodgings carrying a bent bicycle, a crumpled backpack, and some bewildering memories.

The seminary of evangelical theology at Montpellier had its own unique atmosphere. The mountain range of the Cévennes, which lay nearby, had been the center of Protestant resistance during the years of persecution under Louis XIV. On a visit to the wild coastal country of the Camargue, where the bulls are bred for fighting, I was shown the Tour de Constance, where Huguenot women had been imprisoned, and I saw the word "Résistez" carved into the wall, the work of a woman of the Reformed faith who had been kept there for forty years. That spirit was still alive. (I believe a disproportionate number of Protestant French later enrolled in another

---

*The Church of the Holy Family (Templo Expiatorio de La Sagrada Familie, begun in the 1880s by Antonio Gaudi and unfinished today)

movement of resistance, including some who were my fellow students here.) In 1932 the students there were not exactly militant, but it was the most conservative of the three seminaries in France. I was made to feel at home right away—everybody used the informal "tu" when addressing each other—and I soon discovered that theology there was enlivened by the flow of wit, gaiety, and practical jokes. Certain things surprised me at first: the luscious figs that lay untouched on the ground, the exotic dishes like aubergines, the wine that flowed with the meals, the "tartine," as they called it, which was nothing more than bread and jam. In the afternoon I was often invited to enjoy this delicacy, washed down with what they claimed to be tea, in the company of a select group of students. It was only later that I discovered that every group like this had a particular theological stance. Some were strongly pietistic, even fundamentalist; others were distinctly liberal; and a new group was whispered to be "Barthien." This was, I think, the first time I heard the name that would come to mean so much to the theological world—and to me. It is forever linked in my mind with the next revolution in my religious development.

It was announced one day that Pierre Maury was coming to the seminary to conduct a retreat. We all gathered in the biggest classroom in a spirit of theological excitement. We knew Maury was a disciple of the great Karl Barth, and was coming directly from Bonn, where the master taught. He was later to be known as one of France's greatest preachers, and known worldwide as a leader of the ecumenical movement. He was tall, broad-shouldered, lively, and on fire with his theme. I sat spellbound. It has since struck me as a stroke of luck that I first heard the theology of Barth mediated to me in the French language, for at least I thought I was understanding it. One of our professors in Edinburgh had translated the philosophy of Kant into English, and the legend was that even German students read the English version to know what was being said. German is such a wonderful language in which to be obscure. Be that as it may (I would much rather read Shakespeare in German than in French), the thinking of Barth as Maury explained it was for me electrifying.

I have been trying to understand what happened to me

then. Somehow I felt that God was reaching into me in a new way. As I have indicated, the only reason I had clung to a narrow way of understanding the Bible and a set of doctrines that I had really outgrown was that I was convinced that outside these restricted circles I had been moving in lay the wasteland of a shallow liberalism where the gospel of the crucified and risen Christ disappeared into the shifting sands of a tepid "morality tinged with emotion"—and at that time I had a foolish scorn for Matthew Arnold and all his ways. Although I was rebelling more and more against the pietistic taboos I have described, I still had qualms about deserting them entirely. Now here was Maury and behind him the magnetic figure of Barth—two men who spoke of God in all his glory with a far greater power than the fundamentalists (whose God tended to be as narrow as the range of their own imaginations); who spoke of God's Word in language so dynamic that it shattered my previous concept of the Bible as a codebook of doctrines and morals plus a few stories and passages of dramatic power; who lifted up Christ in his incarnation, death, and resurrection as the unique Savior and Lord of a fallen world; and who obviously were able to accept the critical view of the Scriptures not grudgingly but joyfully, as a sign of the true humanity through which God speaks. The great theologian Maury was explaining was also the man with the much-beloved pipe (to which he makes so many affectionate references in his letters), who clearly indulged with gusto in what my previous mentors had labeled "worldly amusements."

Many people today may find it curious that Karl Barth affected me so profoundly, but I have discovered that I was by no means the only one during these years, and since, to find in this theology an escape from the false dilemma in which my generation was ensnared. It was a liberation. It didn't matter now if previous Christian companions should label me a backslider or whisper that I was no longer "keen." I felt keener than ever. But what surprised me most about this latest battle in my own private theological war was not that I escaped from the horns of a dilemma on which I should never have been impaled, but that I experienced a spiritual

ecstasy during those days in Montpellier as intense as any
before or since. It would, I am sure, have pained Barth (though
not Maury) to think that his theology should have triggered
one of my most vivid mystical experiences, for he was intensely suspicious of mysticism in any form. The fact remains
that I spent some days in a state in which I not only was
theologically intoxicated but felt a new and overwhelming
spirit of adoration and communion with God in Christ. I remember bounding up the stairs to my bedroom shouting, at
least inwardly, "Glory to God in the highest!" The Word of
this God was no longer locked in an infallible book of instructions. It spoke to me with the *Hic et Nunc* ("Here and Now")
of the Holy Spirit. I knew now what had struck me that night
in Charlotte Chapel when I received the call to the ministry.
It is not surprising that for the rest of my theological course
I was a fervid Barthian—at least until I learned that the great
man himself repudiated the term, and until other mentors
came along to modify what was becoming my slavish ad-
herence to his views. To this day, however much I may have
deviated from what we foolishly considered Barthian orthodoxy (he himself never thought there was such a thing), and
however much I have been influenced by John Baillie, Reinhold Niebuhr, and even Paul Tillich—not to mention Dietrich
Bonhoeffer, Karl Rahner, and Hans Kung—Karl Barth remains
for me *the* theologian of the twentieth century. And I salute
the memory of Pierre Maury, the lively and courageous
Frenchman who introduced me to him.

The next stop on my theological tour was Strasbourg.
Coming from the warm geographical and theological climate
of the Midi to the rigors and tensions of Alsace was a shock
to my system. My few months at the "Stift," as the Protestant
seminary attached to the University of Strasbourg was called,
opened my eyes to political, religious, and social tensions that
I had never dreamed of before. Gone was the cosy, affectionate, evangelical atmosphere of Montpellier with its moments
of gaiety and theological bliss. The first suggestion of how
different Strasbourg would be was my welcome to the seminary: I was told that this was the theological home of Albert
Schweitzer, that my attendance at classes would be sternly

checked, and that on no account must I bring any girls into my room. Then I became aware of the principal tension there. Strasbourg had been claimed by the French before 1870, then had been claimed by the Germans until 1918, when it had reverted to France. I realized that during these upheavals the Alsatians preferred to be just that—Alsatians—and they resented the ruling bureaucracy imported from either Berlin or Paris. The churches, which were mainly of Lutheran origin, tended to resist the French influence and were consequently suspected by the authorities of "autonomism." The few students who came from the French interior did not have much to do with the native Alsatians.

I discovered the second major tension at the same time I discovered the first one. There were as many foreigners as French at the seminary, and at meals we sat alternately, a foreigner and an Alsatian. The Alsatians carried on their conversation in their special dialect and more or less ignored the rest of us. But the rest of us were by no means a happy band of brothers. I soon discovered that a Hungarian would hardly speak to a Slovak, an Italian detested a Yugoslav, a Romanian disliked the company of a Hungarian, a Czech watched a German suspiciously—and so on, with innumerable complications. I mustn't exaggerate. There were occasional convivial parties between students of different nationalities. But underneath such gestures were these constant tensions. The first month I was there the police swooped in and removed a German who was charged with espionage. When Schweitzer honored us with a visit, the dean, who was a Frenchman from the interior, delivered a polite speech of welcome in French, whereupon our visitor grunted a few words in reply and then retired to chatter happily with the Alsatians.

For the first time I was being exposed to the rivalries and hatreds that had torn Europe apart for centuries. I began to understand how fearful wars could erupt easily out of "incidents"—for instance, the assassination of an Austrian archduke in Serbia in 1914. I was made to see that future conflicts were not going to be averted by the thousands in Britain who were wearing buttons proclaiming "War—We Say NO!" One evening I went to see Remarque's *All Quiet on the Western Front*. I was deeply moved by it, and later asked a Hungarian friend if he had seen it. "No," he said, "it's pacifist propaganda. We are not pacifists. Only those who won the war can afford to be pacifists." That made me think. On another occasion I was leaning over a railing in the gallery that looks down on the main hall of the university, chatting with another Hungarian friend. Below us students were pacing around, talking their heads off. Several Roman Catholic seminarians in long black cassocks were pacing back and forth. I was fascinated by their habit of walking in threes, each trio facing another, so that half of them were always walking backwards. Suddenly my companion spoke. "The future of our world," he said, "will be determined by one of three forces—Catholicism, Communism, or Calvinism." The remark is, of course, dated, but I have often reflected on it. While we were studying in Strasbourg, Hitler had come to power (on the last day of January that year). But my friend, whose country was to be racked by both Nazis and Communists, evidently saw through the threat of the "Thousand Year Reich" and ignored the Nazis as doomed to disappear. These were the topics we pondered and discussed on Sunday afternoon walks to the Rhine bridge. On our side we heard the machine guns practicing from the outworks of the Maginot Line, and on the other side of the bridge we saw the new swastikas fluttering over Kehl.

Once I had assimilated some of the underlying currents of conflict in Strasbourg, the city became for me a wonderful place in which to live and make friends. I grew to love its cathedral, its winding streets, and its cafés with their odor of beer and sauerkraut. And I was increasingly drawn into warm and lively relationships with my fellow students. We argued interminably—Barthians against liberals, High Churchmen against Low Churchmen, Lutherans against Calvinists, Christian socialists against conservatives, ardent democrats against those who were attracted to the Hitler image. I remember more of them than I can possibly describe. There was the Norwegian, Prenter, who subsequently became one of the great Lutheran theologians in the ecumenical world. There was Merjeiovski, a Czech who endured the agonies of his country, worked for a while in Geneva with the World Council of Churches, and whom I last saw (by what a Calvinist can never call "chance") in Prague a few years ago when I was visiting with the Appeal of Conscience delegation; he gave me valuable insights into the religious situation there. There was Bouzalka, a Slovak whom I met in the late thirties when I was wandering through central Europe. I visited him in his barracks, where he was wearing the uniform of the doomed Czech army. I saw him once again in Paris; then came a letter after the Munich conference in which he poured out the agony of his soul, which I matched with the fearful disturbance of my own at that time. There was Bouyer, the most brilliant student of us all, who is now a Jesuit theologian with a world-wide reputation. There was van der Flier, the Dutchman with whom I was very close, who went to a parish in Holland, lived through the occupation, and then died at an early age. Then there was Pavel, the Romanian who was studying the ethics of Saint Augustine when he wasn't arguing with Rostagno, the Italian Waldensian. I mention that because they had the rooms on either side of me, and would talk back and forth from them, so I dropped off to sleep at night with their fluent—if diverse—French ringing in my ears. In 1982 I enjoyed a reunion with Pavel in Bucharest. As we shared our experiences of the last fifty years, he told me that throughout the German occupation he had dodged military service and gone on studying Saint Augustine; when the Communists came, he survived and went on with his studies, eventually becoming Professor of Moral Theology at the Orthodox Seminary in Bucharest.

"What are you doing now?" I asked.

He smiled. "I've retired, but this year I have finally got permission to print my book"—and he showed me the two volumes of his treatise on the ethics of Saint Augustine.

I discovered that several of the prominent churchmen in Romania had been fellow students of mine in Strasbourg—including the present patriarch.

Next stop: Paris. This was a city already familiar to me—more familiar than Glasgow, where I always got lost, and more familiar than London, which was foreign territory for me. I had gone to Paris as a schoolboy and had explored the city with friends on student vacations. As I mentioned earlier, I had also made frequent trips there with my father. We would have breakfast at eight in a bistro, then spend the day walking through the narrow streets rich with history. We would have a final drink around midnight, usually at the Café Regence, where my father would play chess with the expert players who were regulars there. In the center of the café was the glistening table, carefully preserved, where Napoleon used to play. We would stay at some little hotel where at night if you pressed the button labeled "minuterie," sixty seconds' worth of light flashed on to show you up the creaky stairs. We usually didn't make it in the allotted minute, and we would flounder in the darkness to our room.

The Faculté de Theologie Protestante on the Boulevard Arago turned out to be totally different from those of Montpellier and Strasbourg. Paris had absorbed it into its atmosphere of sophistication and sparkle, and we foreigners were soon embraced in its special camaraderie—not so cosy and intimate as that of Montpellier, and not so politicized as that of Strasbourg. For some it was a time of considerable theological ferment. For many years the seminary had been dominated by a liberal school that had produced some giants of theological erudition. Two of our professors also taught at the Sorbonne and had worldwide reputations—Maurice Goguel in the New Testament chair, who was the author of *La Vie de Jesus*, which was already a classic; and Adolphe Lods, a distinguished Old Testament scholar. But strong winds were now blowing from Bonn, and John Calvin, whose works had lain on the shelf for decades, was coming into his own again for a new generation of students—with little encouragement from the professors. I discovered that a great Calvin scholar, Auguste Lecerf, had found a niche in the teaching staff that was supposed to keep him out of mischief. He was employed to teach the English language. Word soon came to me that although presumably I didn't need this kind of instruction, I should attend his class. I soon learned why. He was using as a textbook James Jeans' *The Mysterious Universe*, and would usually begin by asking a student to read a paragraph. After correcting the student's pronunciation, he would immediately seize on some philosophical or scientific point Jeans was making, repeat it in French, and then launch into a thorough theological critique along strictly Calvinist lines. Lecerf also took groups of us on a pilgrimage to Noyon, where Calvin was born, and we basked in his enthusiasm for his theological hero.

In general, we talked nonstop in our rooms and in the corridors, and read voraciously—especially when we could get hold of works by Barth, either in German or in translation. We were stimulated by rumors of Church resistance to Hitler inspired by the neo-orthodox theology, and were attracted to or repelled by the dominant Roman Catholicism. We absorbed some of the current French cynicism about all politicians, and debated the issues of war and peace. Most of the French students had done their stint of military service (two years—or was it three?), and there was agonizing debate about "objection de conscience." Were we aware of what was being prepared for us across the Rhine? I don't know. Although many saw the Barthian movement as a great hope for the renewal of the Protestant churches and, indeed, of Western democracy, which was apparently in its death throes, our contempt for what we called the "old liberals" was met by the riposte that our passion for orthodox and authoritarian creeds was just another example of the extremism and dogmatism that possessed the youth that were hailing Mussolini and Hitler. My newfound faith in the sovereign God, ruler of history, his judgment and mercy mediated to us through the crucified and risen Christ, and my new passion to hear and deliver the dynamic Word in the power of the Spirit—these were for me the lodestars that would guide us through what Winston Churchill was to call "the gathering storm."

After some excursions, such as a weekend spent at scout camp at Rambouillet (where I discovered that French schoolboys had much in common with their Scots counterparts and even knew the same jokes), visits to ancient sites, and religious enterprises connected with both Protestants and Catholics, I left for home. Before saying good-bye to the many friends I had made (some of whom didn't survive the coming war, others of whom I still hear from), I decided to make a final expedition through the streets of Paris—this time an all-night affair. Looking around for an equally crazy companion, I settled for a Dutchman named Kropp, who thought it was a splendid idea. Kropp was a strong-minded eccentric who stood aloof from most of our theological chatter. He wore a beard, which was a rarity in the student world of those days, and whenever he had any money he spent it in restaurants the rest of us couldn't afford. After planning our exit and return to the seminary so that our absence would go unobserved, we set off to walk right through Paris to a movie theater on the Boulevard Clichy. (Yes, I know that it's the notorious nightclub district, but with our limited funds we could manage only the price of a movie.) We emerged from the theater after midnight, wandered through the throngs of late revelers, and then walked along deserted streets, arguing with each other and with occasional strangers in any café that was open. For better or for worse, I have no sensational incident to relate. What I remember is how peaceful the city was—peaceful, that is, until about four in the morning, when we came to the great boulevards that led toward Les Halles, the market area. Down the empty streets came huge horse-drawn wagons piled with vegetables, fruit, carcasses, and chickens. It was as though we had been transported to the French countryside. We had a bowl of the onion soup for which the district is renowned and chatted with any farmer who was not too busy. Finally we reached the bottom of the Avenue de l'Opera, wondering if we still had the energy to walk the few miles back to the seminary with no money left for even a frugal French breakfast. It was then that we met an atheist taxi-driver, who was very eloquent and charming and seemed delighted to spend an idle hour before his early-morning business picked up. We debated the existence of God vigorously for a while, and then discovered that he had never met a Protestant before. We undertook his instruction, and when we were finished he grinned and offered to give us a free ride back to the Boulevard Arago. I remember Kropp as a good companion that night; I have wondered how he later fared in the parish in Rotterdam where he was rumored to be going, or indeed whether, with his temperament, he even survived the occupation. The memory of the taxi driver reminds me that an atheist can be kind.

When I returned to Edinburgh, with its familiar sights, sounds, and odors, I experienced culture shock in reverse, but soon I was enveloped in the life of New College, which was part of the Department of Divinity at the university. Looking back, I realize that the arrival of my class was something of a shock to the old inhabitants of that theological world. To begin with, there were forty-two of us, far more than the usual number. In addition, there was a high proportion of honors students, and among them nearly all were already—or were about to become—Barthian, neo-Calvinist, or neo-orthodox. The theology of the others ranged from the vague to the fundamentalist. For years the tone of the teaching had been what might be called liberal-evangelical, and most of the students had been just plain liberal. With our arrival came a changing of the guard: some great scholars were retiring. One was A. R. S. Kennedy, whose name can be found at the end of many scholarly articles on Old Testament themes in many volumes and encyclopedias. His wife was passionately involved in evangelical causes and had a rigorous fundamentalist attitude toward the Bible. Kennedy, who wore a skullcap, was known as Torah. He would finish expounding the documentary hypothesis concerning the Pentateuch—which was news to many of us—with great skill and erudition, then finish with a grin, saying, "These, gentlemen, are the generally accepted views of the scholars, but my wife doesn't believe a word of them." Adam Welch, another Old Testament scholar, whose views on the composition of the Book of Deuteronomy were discussed on several continents, could rise to moments of great oratory and emotion when dealing with favorite characters like King Saul. On occasion he would also interject pithy remarks into his scholarly discourse, such as "The curse of the ministry is laziness." W. P. Paterson, who held the Chair of Divinity, was another intellectual giant. His absent-mindedness spawned dozens of legends. (According to one story he had once telephoned his wife from a railway station in the middle of Scotland and said, "My dear, I'm in Perth.

Where am I going?") In his later years he wrote with the kind of clarity and simplicity that comes only after the obscurities have been waded through.

The teacher who made the profoundest impression on us at that time was H. R. Mackintosh, and his sudden death in our last year was a great blow to us all. His book, *The Doctrine of the Person of Jesus Christ,* was for a long time required reading in seminaries all over Britain, the Continent, and the United States. We were deeply affected not only by his scholarship but by his faithfulness to what we felt were the essential doctrines of the historic Catholic faith, his sense of the holy, and his evangelical zeal. His lectures generated an unusual spirit of worship even among those of us who were known to interject flippant comments or create disturbances in other lecture rooms. (But he was by no means inhumanly serious; he once surprised me in private conversation by remarking, "You know, your generation is much more devout than ours: we used to play bridge in the back seats when old 'So-and-So' was lecturing.") Of course, what we loved about Mackintosh was his growing interest in Barth, whom he encouraged us to read.

It was not so with our principal, William Curtis, a man of infinite kindness, who had an encyclopedic knowledge of almost any subject you liked to raise—from ecclesiastical politics to insect life. He was famous for beginning a complex sentence, when expounding John's Gospel, and finishing it grammatically and impeccably about five minutes later. We always applauded the best of these. Curtis was adamantly opposed to our attraction to Barth, whom he considered theologically lopsided, an obscurantist who would lead us to repudiate centuries of rational and richly humanist Scottish theology. At the end of my first year I discovered that among his skills was procuring various funds that he used to send promising students to study in Europe. So I immediately told him that I wanted to learn German in order to pursue my theological studies and would dearly like to spend the summer there.

"Where do you want to go?" he asked.

"Bonn," I said at once.

"You will not go to Bonn," he said firmly.

A few days later he telephoned me and asked, "How would you like to go to Marburg?"

I agreed immediately, thinking that at least there I would hear Rudolf Otto, whose book, *The Idea of the Holy*, was enormously influential; in it he discusses the "numinous" and the *Mysterium tremendum et fascinans*, which greatly appealed to me. There was also another Rudolf there—Rudolf Bultmann, who was gaining a reputation as a controversial and original New Testament scholar. But details of this experience must come later.

Thus we had a rich variety of professors to enlarge our horizons and with whom to argue when we disagreed. William Manson, who was not only a first-class New Testament exegete but, in my opinion, a saint, was one of those to whom I should have listened with far greater attention. I go back now to his commentary on Luke, for instance, and wonder why I spent occasional moments during his lectures devising stupid games to while away the time or inscribed disrespectful limericks on the desk in front of me when I could have been absorbing so much more of his insight and scholarship.

It would be tiresome to list name after name of my contemporaries who subsequently embarked on remarkable careers as professors of theology, church statesmen, ecumenical leaders, and pulpit personalities. We had vigorous discussions and enjoyed some uproarious times together. Somehow the new theological stream was carrying a great variety of temperaments toward what our elders called this "Barthian bug." We used to debate the seminarians from Glasgow, where Barth didn't seem to have a single follower, and cross swords with the Episcopalians, who were much more interested in liturgical matters. (I remember taking two volumes of Calvin's *Institutes* to those debates to intimidate the opposition.) With all this went our search, common to most generations of seminarians, for a more active spiritual life in the college. We had short prayers every day at eleven o'clock, but that didn't satisfy us. One incident that occurred in connection with this quest taught me a lesson I'll never forget—that perfectly sincere Christians can express their faith in ways that are mutually unacceptable. One day, after much debate about spirituality, we decided that all we could do was to meet in a room in a corner of the building and spend half an hour in prayer, each praying as he felt led. At first there was a very long silence. Then one of our most earnest souls, a man of strong evangelical persuasion, launched into a lengthy appeal in which he implored the Lord to enlighten and convert those of us who he felt had not been truly converted. When his impassioned—and totally informal—pleas had ceased, there was a pause. Then another voice was heard: "Almighty God, unto whom all hearts are open. . . ." When he finished, our prayer time was over, never to be resumed in that form. Later each of these two friends came to see me separately.

"David," said the earnest one, referring to the other, "did you hear him? That cold, gabbled collect. He doesn't know the Lord."

"David," said the other about the first speaker, "wasn't that absolutely shocking the way he went on? That was sheer blasphemy."

Chapter Six

WAITING
FOR
HITLER

A new man appeared on this turbulent theological scene. The successor to W. P. Paterson as the Regius Professor of Divinity was the formidable John Baillie, who had returned from the United States to his native land. Years later he confided to me that the adjustment was rather bewildering. At Union Seminary in New York the students had considered him a pillar of orthodoxy, whereas we treated him like a stimulating heretic on whose arguments we could cut our theological teeth. Looking back, I realize that both John and his brother Donald at St. Andrew's were among the most devout and brilliant theologians of this generation. John's book *Our Knowledge of God* and Donald's *God Was in Christ* have been influential throughout the Christian world. They both published sermons, along with other theological works, which demonstrate that a professor can also be a preacher. According to tradition in Scotland the usual way to a seminary chair was through service in a parish. John was an exception to this rule, but he never lost contact with the life of the ordinary parish church. Thus Scotland—at least in those days—never produced the kind of theological thinker who pursues his studies in isolation from the ongoing life of Christian congregations. It is not so in the United States, where promising seminarians have been encouraged to proceed into the oceans of academic theology without wetting their feet in the parish where the Holy Catholic Church takes visible form. Evanescent aberrations like the "Death of God" theology are unlikely to appear among theologians who have spent some time with congregations for whom he is very much alive.

Baillie had a wide-ranging intellect with which he distilled theological thought with beautiful clarity. He had a great affection for the classics, particularly Plato. (Here I have to confess authorship of a little ditty we began to sing while awaiting his appearance. It was set to a well-known tune, and began, "Baillie, Baillie, give me your answer, do: Why ain't Plato found in the canon, too?") He had an unusual approach for a professor: he asked us to interrupt him if we didn't follow him or wanted to contradict him—a request of which we took full advantage. Once, after he had expounded and strongly criticized the chapter in the Westminster Confession headed "Of the Fall of Man, of Sin, and of the Punishment Thereof," he called on me to explain it. I said something to the effect that I found nothing wrong with it. He then quoted the statement that men are "wholly defiled in all the faculties and parts of soul and body." If man was totally depraved, he asked, how could he possibly know it? This was one of a number of times that Calvinism was given a sharp jolt by Baillie's incisive mind. For some years now, if I want a quick answer to the question of my theology, the phrase I use is "Barth modified by Baillie."

The occupant of a peculiar chair dealing with the relationship of science and religion was J. Y. Simpson, a distinguished and charming scholar and diplomat. The chair dated from the time of the brilliant evangelist Henry Drummond and the creation/evolution debates of those days. We were by no means anxious to revive that question on the old terms (or perhaps I should say "new," since it has raised its ugly head again), but we were intolerant of any attempts to square the findings of science with the doctrines of the faith. When confronted with the question "Does Science leave room for God?" on the end-of-term examination, I began by remarking that it was the wrong question, the right one being "Does God leave room for this kind of Science?" and went on from there.

This Chestertonian quip did me no good in the exam results—and rightly so. I must have been equally insufferable the time that I objected violently when Simpson referred to the doctrine of the damnation of unbaptized infants as "this wretched Calvinism." In Scotland it is the habit for students to drum their feet on the floor when they appreciate what the professor is saying, and to shuffle them when they disagree. As I was the leading shuffler on this occasion, the professor asked me whether I also held to this doctrine. I replied, "No, sir—and neither did Calvin," citing the chapter in the *Institutes* in which Calvin vehemently repudiates such teaching. It was typical that the following day "J.Y.," as we called him, announced that he had looked the matter up, that I was right, and that, in fact, he had never read the *Institutes*. I don't know whether we were more shocked by his admission or impressed by his magnanimity. He was invariably so patient, kind, and lovable that it was a great joy to me, on coming to Madison Avenue Presbyterian Church twenty years later, to find his widow an active member of our congregation.

The interlude in Marburg, Germany, during the summer of 1934 was an additional stimulus to my theological and political development. I was there chiefly to learn the language and become generally familiar with current theology and the burgeoning Church struggle with the Nazi state. I should note that at this time we had a much clearer idea of the position of Karl Barth than that of Adolf Hitler. I began to learn how closely theology and politics can sometimes be interwoven. Both Britain and the United States were unsure of the nature and intentions of the National Socialist Party. Churchill's insights had not yet begun to influence us, and even among Scottish students there was debate about whether or not Hitler would turn out to be a "good thing."

I found lodgings with a couple of warmhearted ladies from Saxony who looked after their two Scots guests with motherly attention and succeeded in keeping two very militaristic German students from being too arrogant at the dining table. When I asked one of the ladies privately one day what she thought of Hitler, she simply said, "I don't know anything about politics, but I do know that since Hitler came it's been safe to go out in the streets." I have often thought about that remark when hearing talk about "It couldn't happen here." After all, safe streets are more important to most people than trains that run on time.

My Scottish companion, who was also from Edinburgh (and who later spent years as a missionary in India), and I were joined twice a week by two German students from the university. One was in the S.A. and the other in the S.S., and they were supposed to teach us German to supplement the lessons we were taking from an old lady who was the widow of a World War I general. She represented the fierce but conscientious militarism of the past; the students gave me a premonition of the totally unscrupulous militarism of the new generation. All of our discussions were jovial, but occasionally something gave me a glimpse of what we might soon be up against. One day I asked for the words to some songs that I had heard the young Nazis singing in the street, and one of our companions brought me a sheaf of lyrics. Some were good old German drinking songs, but among them I came across one that reeked of the crudest anti-Semitism, talking of the great day when "Jewish blood would run in the gutters." The very next day my companion returned with a pair of scissors, solemnly asked to have the songs back, and proceeded to cut out these offending verses. Nothing, of course, could have made it more certain that I would remember them. On another day we attended a splendid performance of *A Midsummer Night's Dream* in German given on the perfect natural stage up by the Schloss. On our way there we passed a group of storm troopers carrying the Nazi banner. Suddenly a giant figure stepped right in front of me and roared, "Warum haben Sie die Fahne nicht gegrüsst?" I explained that I was a foreigner and heard the word passed along: "No fuss: Englander!" In spite of the inaccuracy I didn't bother to contradict him. I just wondered how I would have fared if I had been German—and Jewish.

One more incident again made me think of the evils that were surely lurking behind the outward gaiety, enthusiasm, and discipline of this Nazi youth. One night another Scottish friend came to see us in some distress. It seemed that he had

been waiting for a train at a country station when a group of
S.A. men arrived carrying a large wooden box. They left the
box on the platform and went off for a drink. As our friend
watched he saw, to his horror, a live human arm protrude for
a moment, then slip back into the box. That was all. I began
to see these attractive German youngsters in a new light. Then
came the memorable "Night of the Long Knives"—the time
when Hitler decided to liquidate the S.A. leaders, including
the notorious Ernst Röhm, whom he personally shot when he
and his cronies were having a drunken party one June night.
We were perplexed. The German press made little of the event,
simply noting that the Führer had fortunately learned of a plot
to overthrow the regime and had nipped it in the bud. Some
dozen names of the executed were listed. Only later did we
know the full extent of the bloodletting that night. As we met
for church the next morning, one of the Scottish students went
so far as to say that he was enormously relieved that the attempt had been crushed and felt like saying "Heil Hitler!" for
the first time.

Meanwhile I was attending lectures and gradually picking
up the language. In German universities students are not required to attend lectures; they go to the ones that interest
them. When I attended a class in the afternoon to hear the
world-famous Rudolf Otto, I found just a handful of students
present. Otto was not "in," as we say today. The next morning
I went at 7:30 to hear Rudolf Bultmann and found a room
packed with about four hundred students. Theologians' pop-
ularity, I learned, varied with the prevailing theological wind,
and I began to realize that just because we were caught up in
the neo-orthodox frenzy, it was not necessarily the only truth,
and would not last forever. I didn't understand much of what
Bultmann was saying, but I did notice that he opened his
lecture with the most perfunctory "Heil Hitler" I had ever
heard. (The greeting was mandatory for all lecturers, and
Barth's refusal to give it even perfunctorily was one reason
why he left Bonn.) I learned more about the growing tensions
in the German Church, and of the growing movement that
was to culminate that year in the Confession of Barmen, in
which several Nazi doctrines were deliberately repudiated as

contrary to the lordship of Christ. We knew all this was highly dangerous, but the students who stood by the strong doctrines they had learned from Barth were extraordinarily courageous. Word would filter through that Barth was to be preaching that Sunday in Bonn, and a whole party would set out to hear him, cycling through the night to get there.

At the end of my Marburg term I was seized again by wanderlust, and I set off to travel as cheaply as possible to Munich, Vienna, Prague, Bratislava, Dresden, Berlin, and Hamburg—and so home. In Munich I met a nephew of my Marburg landladies who showed me around. I mention him here because after the war when I revisited Marburg I took some chocolate and soap to my old landladies, and in the course of relating my adventures as a P.O.W. in Germany, I discovered that her nephew had been a guard in my last prison camp, and was thus taken prisoner on the day I was released. What I remember about Vienna is standing and gazing at an imposing old building on which were inscribed the words "Si Vis Pacem, para bellum." An old gentleman in a straw hat watched me and then remarked quietly, "Yes, we prepared for war—and we got it. It's going to happen again." I felt more sure of the truth of that remark when, in Dresden the next day, I was arrested by an S.A. guard at the Schloss because I was taking photographs. I was hustled to the commandant's office, where I explained that I saw no harm in photographing the S.A., as it had been explained to me that they were really a group something like the Boy Scouts. As I spoke I noticed the racks of rifles that were never seen in the streets. My British passport calmed my interrogator (at that time the Nazis were all instructed to be very polite to British and American visitors). He began to smile, but when his eye caught the stamps that revealed my speedy journey from Marburg through Munich to Vienna (and also a trip I had taken down the Danube to Bratislava), he got wildly excited, and the next thing I knew I was put in an armored car headed for the Gestapo headquarters. Since I knew that my story was true and that they had their instructions to go easy on the Anglo-Saxons, I was not too anxious. Neither was my traveling companion, Cowie, my placid scientific friend whom I had met by prearrangement in Dresden. So the incident ended with apologies and smiles. But once again I wondered what would have happened if I had been German—and a Jew.

The day after I had left Vienna, Chancellor Dollfuss had been murdered by the Nazis, so excitement was running high in both Dresden and Berlin. More and more I was feeling the sinister pressure behind the outward enthusiasms of the new German. It is very tempting now to say that I was certain war would come, that I was being summoned by God to play my part in whatever steps the democracies would finally take to resist them, that I was fully aware of the fact that my friends in the Confessing Church were about to risk their lives in Christ's name. The truth is that I detested the thought of war and managed to convince myself that if the democracies stood firm and rearmed, there would be no fighting (a proposition that may very well have been right). At that point I was not ready to throw myself into active anti-Nazi agitation. I had not yet taken full account of the theological dimension of the growing ideological conflict, and I returned to Edinburgh sure of only one thing—that nothing would interfere with God's call to me to be a preacher. I was right, but the way in which God would amplify that call was, perhaps fortunately, still hidden from me.

New College continued to be a stimulating place. There we wrestled with old doctrines and strange new thoughts; were highly critical of the churches as we knew them compared to our vision of the Holy Catholic Church, the Body of Christ on earth; argued interminably about theology, liturgy, and missions; delighted in exegesis; and were often bogged down in the mysteries of Hebrew grammar. Except for those of us who had resolved to keep their religious opinions intact while passing the necessary examination that would lead to ordination, we were constantly wrestling with new ideas, being shaped, consciously or unconsciously, by stimulating teachers—and by one another. Labels like "conservative," "liberal," "High Church," "Low Church," "Auld Kirk," and "U.F." came to mean less and less. Some of us had entered seminary with the thought of becoming preachers foremost in our minds, and were not much concerned with such matters as liturgy, order, and the historic Catholic tradition in which the Church of Scotland stood. Others were passionately concerned with that tradition and with the revival of a strong sacramental worship in Presbyterianism. Still others were content to leave matters of doctrine and liturgy to the higher authorities while they concentrated on the impact of the Church on society and the battle against poverty, injustice, and war. There were very few who were content to slip through seminary undisturbed by any of these concerns on their way to some quiet parish where life would go on as it had for centuries past. As chairman of the Divinity Students Council, my job was usually to preside over our boisterous meetings. But I once had to represent to the teaching staff our views on everything from the heating system in the college and the provision for our hours of recreation to the poverty of our spiritual life, the overemphasis on examinations, and (very diplomatically) the inadequacy of some of the lectures. I proposed to summarize all these things as being "antipathetic to the ethos of New College," but was properly shouted down by my peers. Our elders and mentors listened patiently, and life went on as usual. In spite of this exhilarating experience of leadership in our modest version of the "corridors of power," I decided within the next few years that church politics was not for me. I have always been glad that some delight in church law and the machinery of our Presbyterian polity, but only occasionally have I felt any desire to give time and energy to matters of procedure, to attempt to sway presbyteries or assemblies, and I have never nourished moderatorial ambitions.

I was, however, grateful for the administrative skills of people like Principal Curtis, whose financial wizardry now unearthed funds to give some fortunate students an opportunity to visit the Holy Land. Thus in the spring of 1935 eight of us embarked on a ship that took us across a stormy Bay of Biscay to Port Said and thence to Cairo; eventually we boarded a train that puffed its way up the slopes from Jaffa to Jerusalem. These six weeks in what was then called Palestine (then under the British mandate from the League of Nations) were unforgettable. The situation then was not unlike that of biblical times. We stayed at the hospice attached to the Church of Scotland, charge of St. Andrew's, and on Sunday the lessons in church were read by a notable Scotsman who occupied roughly the same position as Pontius Pilate had. Trouble came from both Arab and Jewish groups, and there was visible tension not only between Jews, Christians, and Moslems but between the many Christian churches that laid claim to the holy sites. The occupying power, naturally, was the vortex to which the disputes were drawn. Once again I had to adjust my thinking about the nature of the gospel to which I was committed, the true life of the Holy Church, which was coming to mean more and more to me, and the impossibility, as a Christian, of opting out of political decisions.

We students were divided in our reactions to all that we saw. Some were highly skeptical, as we explored the land, of the claims that we stood on the "actual spot" where Abraham was buried or Jesus was born, and were almost Bultmannian in their rejection of the historicity of many Bible stories. Others devoutly joined in any available procession of pilgrims, kissed holy relics, and were attracted to the piety of the Eastern Orthodox. Some were evangelicals who were appalled by the sight of an image of the Virgin Mary hung with trinkets and wristwatches, and spoke sadly of a paganized and debased Christianity that needed the "pure milk of the Word." I myself was moved by much in the devotions of the pilgrims, although I found the commercialization of the holy sites distressing.

Some moments come back to me with special vividness. One day I was walking alone on the Mount of Olives when a young Arab walked past me. He was about thirty years old, and dressed in flowing robes; he had flashing eyes and a dignified walk. He looked as if he had stepped right out of an illustrated children's Bible. Suddenly a thought struck me. "Someone who looked like that walked on this hillside, and we claim that he was no other than the unique Son of God, the Savior of the world. Is it really possible?" In a moment I realized that all the miracle stories of the Bible are really incidental and unimportant compared to this stupendous assertion that God himself walked this earth as such a man. I thought how carelessly we sing our Christmas carols—"Veiled in flesh the Godhead see! Hail the incarnate Deity!" I looked back at the young Arab as he strode down the hill. If I really believed that, other doubts and questions mattered very little. I realized with joy that I did indeed believe it, but I never forgot what the incident said to me about the true humanity as well as the divinity of Jesus, and about the enormousness of the Christian claim. It also left me with a new sympathy for all those who find it so hard to accept.

I remember other moments with similar vividness: floating on the Sea of Galilee and actually seeing "the calm of hills above, where Jesus knelt to share with thee the silence of eternity, interpreted by love," and the contrast of sitting on the Dead Sea (its high salt content buoys up objects, and it takes an effort to get *into* the water); thinking of John the Baptist in his prison in the Castle of Macchaerus above the shore where the Jordan flows in, and being aware again of the "mystery of iniquity" that I had felt that evening with the Nazis by the Marburg Castle. I felt the nearness of Christ when I saw a real leper, when I ate the Galilean fish, when I wandered through the Wilderness of Judea, with its great rocks strewn around as if left over from Creation itself. Our last vivid experience was perching on a precarious balcony in the Church of the Holy Sepulchre, looking down at a sea of worshipers from many lands. They grew wildly excited as the patriarch moved up the aisle, escorted by two stalwart Scottish officers whose job it was to protect him from the enthusiasm of the crowd. Later there came the total silence at midday, when the patriarch entered the tomb of Jesus. Suddenly there was a flash of fire, and in a moment, as the crowd cheered, candles appeared everywhere. Those in the balconies let their candles down on strings so that the entire congregation could share in the holy fire. We left the scene dazzled and bewildered. The symbolism was breathtaking—that holy fire from this tomb of the Resurrection was spreading throughout this vast multitude of Arabs, Europeans, peasants from all over the Middle East, and elegant ladies from near and far. Yet, we wondered, was this really where we were closest to the risen Christ? I loved the scene, but I wasn't sure.

When I returned to Edinburgh, some of the most significant events of my life loomed ahead: getting married, being ordained, and pastoring my first church. Of my marriage I cannot say much, since I have taken a vow of silence at my wife's request—but I must be allowed to say that she was, is, and ever shall be the most important and beloved of all those who have "flowed in" to my life. Of my ordination I have more to say than most people would want to hear, for to me it is a ceremony of the deepest meaning, the confirmation by the Catholic Church of the call that I had personally experienced. We prepared for it by following a series of steps—completing our theological training, being licensed to preach by the Presbytery, and receiving a call to a particular parish that had to be sustained by the ecclesiastical authorities. Before we were licensed we had to preach in a local church in the presence of its minister and one of our seminary professors. I underwent this test on a Sunday evening, faced with a very sparse congregation. After I delivered what I felt to be a truly evangelical sermon on the text of "Looking unto Jesus," devoutly hoping that it was sound enough exegetically for the ears of my professor, I was ushered into the vestry to meet him and the minister. The latter was a jovial type with, I suspected, little interest in the Westminster Confession, on which he was supposed to examine me.

"Let's see," he said, flicking through the pages. "What would you say is the difference between the church visible and the church invisible?"

A wild impulse made me want to reply, "Well, it was certainly invisible tonight, but I hope it was visible this morning."

I restrained myself—unfortunately, I think, since I later learned that he would have appreciated the quip enormously. After a little desultory conversation, we drifted off to drink sherry at the manse. The next day Professor Mackintosh sent for me, and we had a long talk. At one point he asked me, "Were you preaching from a full manuscript and following it loosely—or were you preaching from notes?" I confessed that I had followed my usual custom of having a few notes and talking spontaneously. "Well," he said, "you can do it—but

I recommend to you that when you reach a parish you write out every word of what you are going to say—at least for the morning sermon." I have done so ever since. What moved me more than anything was the final remark he made after tearing the sermon to pieces: "It did my heart good to hear you commend Christ to that congregation."

The process of matching a minister with a particular parish is notoriously difficult, and Scotland has a special name for those who are unable to find churches—"stickit ministers." For about four months I was a "stickit minister," preaching up and down the country as I was needed, determined to pull no strings and convinced that God had his plan for me. Eventually that plan emerged in the form of a call to the smallest of three charges of the Church of Scotland, which was in the famous little town of Coldstream on the banks of the Tweed. It had about 250 members, with about 80 attending on an average Sunday and about 100 on "high holy days." The congregation were the local shopkeepers, farmers and their hired hands, some professional people, and a few retirees. Borderfolk are renowned, even in Scotland, for being dour and uncommunicative. At the time I found them very warm and generous as well as intensely loyal, though when I compare them to American congregations, I would have to confess that they were not demonstrative. During my three years there, the only comment I remember hearing about my preaching was one I got secondhand. I was informed one day after a Harvest Thanksgiving service that the dourest of all our members had been heard to remark, "They'll no' can say oor man canna preach." I treasure that above all other compliments that have ever come my way as a preacher.

Oliver Goldsmith describes his ideal country parson as "passing rich with forty pounds a year." My income at Coldstream was three hundred pounds a year (fifteen hundred dollars at the rate of exchange in the 1930s), and looking back I reckon I was "passing rich," since we had a manse with a garden, a car, and a full-time, live-in maid. Nevertheless, we had to watch our pennies. I remember debating whether I would spend sixpence on a pack of cigarettes or on the *New*

Statesman, a left-wing weekly with which I shared a loathing for the policies of Neville Chamberlain.

Politics colored our life in many ways. At one end of the town was the estate of Lord Home, father of Sir Alec Douglas-Home, on whose waters Mr. Chamberlain came to fish when he should have been keeping his eye on Mr. Hitler. Lord Home was adored by everyone, and all Coldstreamers were welcome to wander about his grounds. At the other end of the town lived a charming and eccentric lady with a rich sense of humor. At her table we met a variety of politicians, both local ones and members of parliament. Discussions of either politics or religion were not barred, and since most of her friends were ardent supporters of Neville Chamberlain, a good time was had by all. She had a butler named Ford and a houseboy named Joseph. Ford, I discovered one day, was on the rolls of my church, and Joseph joined my confirmation class. Shortly after he did so, I met Ford in the street and raised the question of his membership. He quickly changed the subject. "I advised Joseph to join the church," he said solemnly. " 'Joseph,' I said, 'you'd better do it now. You never know when you're going to need a minister.' "

I remember vividly my first visit to this house. Being new to the town, I didn't realize that the grounds adjoined the local golf-course. It was a Sunday, when I normally dressed in frock coat and tall hat. After lunch we strolled through the gardens and came across a tree with a branch hanging loose. My hostess remarked that someone should break it off before it caused trouble. I thereupon took a flying leap at the branch, determined to bring it down. As often happens in these situations, the branch refused to give way, and I was left dangling there, my coattails waving just above a path around the golf course on which I noticed some of my parishioners taking an afternoon stroll (golf, of course, being forbidden on Sunday). I waved politely, and they passed on as if nothing unusual was happening.

My sermons at this time, as I remember them, were solidly biblical, and I gradually learned that theological ideas that had excited me in seminary were not necessarily so thrilling to my rural congregation. However, as I began to understand better what concerned my parishioners in their daily lives, we developed a kind of exchange. I tried to explain to them the practical implications of the gospel, while they taught me how to handle garden tools and care for apple trees, and gently introduced me to the realities of life and the formalities of death. My growing concern with politics led me to that still-perplexing line that separates church and state. In Scotland there was no such thing as that mythical absolute "wall of separation" that we hear so much about in the United States. From Knox onward, the Kirk asserted its right to address the government on all matters affecting morals and religion—often in thunderous tones. Yet as ministers we were trained to avoid saying anything in our sermons that could be interpreted as partisan politics. Both in Coldstream and later in Edinburgh, I don't believe any members of my congregation—except a very few close friends—had any idea of who I voted for in an election. But I have always felt free to declare the Word of God as I heard it on any major social issue.

It was during my years in Coldstream that a single document divided the country from end to end, split apart families, and caused agonizing debates in the Church—the agreement signed at Munich in September 1938. First, it should be noted that the immediate reaction of the majority of British people at the time was relief that war had been avoided. I confess to sharing that feeling for about twenty-four hours. Then I felt sick at heart and ashamed that we had bought a phony peace at the expense of the Czechoslovakian people. It will be argued forever whether or not the time gained for the Allies at Munich was essential for the eventual war that had to be fought. All I can say now is that I reacted by en-listing in the army as a chaplain; I was enrolled in the reserve. Some of my congregation expected a service of thanksgiving for the Munich agreement and were puzzled when I gave no thanks for it but cited the psalm that says, "He gave them their request; but sent leanness into their soul." At that time I happened to meet at one of those dinner parties an M.P. who was an ardent Chamberlain supporter. I asked him point-blank if he thought Chamberlain really believed what he said when he waved the Munich agreement at the airport on his return and announced, "I believe this is peace in our time."

"Of course," he said. "Don't you?"

"Not for a moment," I replied.

He looked solemn, then said, "I hope to God you're not right."

In the spring of 1939 I was asked to represent the Church of Scotland at a small meeting to be held in Emden, Germany, to prepare for a Calvinist conference to be held there in the summer of 1940. Acting on my lifelong principle of never turning down an opportunity to travel, I gladly accepted. Just before we were due to leave, Hitler showed how much he honored the Munich agreement by swallowing up the rest of Czechoslovakia. A professor in Edinburgh who was to have gone with me immediately telephoned and asked, "You're not going to Emden, are you?" I said that I certainly was and set off for Germany via Holland. In Rotterdam I joined another delegate, a Dutch law professor, and we traveled across the Low Country to Emden. As we passed the flatlands around the Zuider Zee, I asked him what would happen if the Germans attacked Holland. "No problem," he said. "We can flood all this territory." I remembered that remark in the spring of 1940. My companion, I learned later, died a victim of the Nazi occupation of Holland.

On arriving at Emden we discovered that we were the only foreigners attending the meeting. We soon got down to business with the help of coffee, beer, and cigars. The German representatives were mostly from the Confessing Church, although one elder there was wearing the Party badge. We stuck to theology and practical arrangements for the conference. It was fascinating to see how the new generation in many countries was reviving Calvinism in modern dress. On the day of my departure I was having a solitary breakfast and reading the *Volkischer Beobachter* when its huge headline caught my eye: DER FUHRER IN WILHELMSHAVEN.

I summoned the waiter. "How far is Wilhelmshaven?"

"About three hours by train," he informed me, "but you can't go there today."

"Why not?"

"Because the only train going is a special excursion of the 'Strength through Joy' movement—and you're a foreigner."

"Could *you* get a ticket?"

When he said yes, I asked him to get me one. So I became a temporary member of the Nazi organization (I still have the badge) and set off for Wilhelmshaven, where Hitler was due to launch a new battleship.

Some hours later I was standing in the front of the crowd that lined the big market square in which Hitler was to speak. Tall S.A. men stood in front of us, every other one turned to face the crowd. Soon the advance guard went roaring past, and then the crowd went wild as an open car drove slowly past with Hitler standing bolt upright in it, gazing at the crowd with a frozen face. I was surprised to see what a pudgy, sallow face he had, and with what contempt he seemed to be looking at us all. He spoke from behind a bulletproof glass screen on the main platform, and gradually worked the crowd up with his usual screeching voice. After the usual celebration of Nazi achievements, he devoted a good part of his speech to Palestine and the iniquities of the British occupation. I was surprised at the relative calmness of the crowd at this point, and when at the end I stood immobile while all other hands were raised, I got some curious stares but no violent looks. On the whole the crowd was good-humored, and a few conversations gave me the impression that not many believed there could be war with Britain. (As one Nazi officer put it later, "With our army and your fleet, we could rule the world!")

Despite the bulletproof screen protecting Hitler, it seemed to me that it would have been easy enough to hurl a bomb at his car in passing. The S.A. guards were too anxious to get a close look to see if any of us was armed. This raises the grim theological question with which Dietrich Bonhoeffer was later to wrestle. If I had gone there with a bomb and killed Hitler, possibly saving millions of lives by doing so, would that have been a Christian act? Would that have been sacrificing one's life to save others? I left for home preoccupied with such thoughts. Passing through London, I stopped to phone my M.P. When he heard that I had been at Wilhelmshaven, he asked me to come around to the House of Commons at once.

He told me that the radio had been cut off in the middle of Hitler's speech and no one knew what he had said—particularly about Palestine. I hurried over, desperately trying to remember the highlights of the speech.

My host in Emden was a local pastor. I remember well his last words to me as I was leaning out of the train window to say good-bye: "Auf Wiedersehen!" he cried. "Be sure to come back to Germany next summer." I did—as a prisoner of war.

Chapter Seven

"IN PRESENCE OF MY FOES"

If anyone had asked me in 1939 what my plans were for my future ministry, I think I should have replied quite honestly that I didn't have any. I had a simple—some would say na-ive—view that the ministry was not the kind of profession in which one mapped out a course to the top; in fact, I found the idea of there being any such thing as a "top" in the min-istry distasteful. Didn't our Lord clearly state that ministry was service, and didn't he rebuke the two disciples who as-pired to the most prestigious places in his coming kingdom? And wasn't the parity of ministers a cardinal principle of Pres-byterian polity in particular? I was also deeply impressed by the concept of the "call," which I interpreted to mean not only my original call to the ministry but every future step in my career. Yet I confess that some kind of picture of my future lurked in the back of my mind. The signs pointed to a short period spent in my first parish, then a call to a larger church, and eventually, perhaps, a call to a big-city parish—or to a chair in theology. All of this I believed to be in the hands of God, but it was difficult for me not to assume that the way ahead was already mapped out for me, because I was already getting occasional unsettling visitors during my services— delegations from other churches (they would carefully hide their tracks by leaving their car across the river and dribbling in singly among the congregation, but my beadle would whisper as he ushered me into the pulpit, "They're from St. So-and-so Glasgow th' morn").

But God had other plans for me, and 1939 turned out to be something very different from another step along what was beginning to look like a predestined path. It began with my first venture into the world of broadcasting and book publishing. My friend from university days, Robert Dunnett, who was now with the BBC, asked me to participate in a series of talks called "The Church I Look For." Knowing nothing about the art of broadcasting, I produced what I thought was a scintillating talk, filled with literary allusions and Chestertonian paradoxes. Dunnett ripped it to pieces, albeit with his usual tact—and taught me how to express simply and directly what I had in mind. The revised piece was published in *The Listener* (the BBC magazine), and soon after that I received a letter from Leonard Cutts of Hodder and Stoughton saying that he had read it and thought that I "had a book in me." The result was what I now consider a premature birth. Since the date of publication coincided with the outbreak of World War II, *The Spirit of Life*, as I had titled it, was not exactly the sensation of the year. Mr. Cutts, who became a lifelong friend and advisor, was not dismayed, and sent me a telegram asking me to translate a book of sermons by Walter Luthi of Basel in about three weeks. My instinct was to refuse because I had only a very sketchy knowledge of German. But my wife pointed out that I would have a much better grasp of it if I did the translation; I agreed, and another book with my name on it appeared during the first week of the war.

With the proceeds from the book (about $120), my wife and I decided to take our ancient, battered car across Europe—as we said, "while it was still there." We crossed Belgium and France to Switzerland, responding to an invitation from Walter Luthi. We met him in Basel, where we talked politics and theology for twenty-four hours. The morning we left was glorious, and I asked our host if we could look forward to radiant weather during our trip through Switzerland and the St. Gotthard Pass to Italy. "Normally," he replied, "I would prophesy fair weather. But I have a strange belief that weather is somehow linked with human events. There's a big storm coming in Europe—so be prepared for anything on your journey." Twelve hours later we were in the midst of a deluge, with thunder rolling through the mountains and lightning flashing over the Swiss lakes. Looking back, I don't know how we crossed the St. Gotthard, which had just been opened to traffic after the snows. Not only was our protection from the rain almost nonexistent, but all our tires were smooth because I couldn't afford new ones. My tolerance of heights was much better then than it is now—which was a good thing, since at the summit I had to back up on the edge of a precipice to let a post-bus pass.

Although we didn't know it, we were within weeks of the outbreak of war, and inklings of that marked our trip: I remember meeting hundreds of troop carriers both in Italy and Germany (we returned by Alsace and a strip of neighboring Germany), and feeling strange because we were out of touch with world news, especially in Italy. We arrived home without incident, but the next three Sundays, which I remember distinctly, suggested imminent change. The pattern was breaking up; life was clearly not going to be moving according to plan. On the first Sunday I broadcast my first sermon, and the occasion was a notable one if only because I had a very bad cold at the time. The next Sunday I fulfilled a memorable engagement. Some months before I had received a letter bearing the royal crest. It was from the minister of Crathie Church, near Balmoral, and his opening words were "I am commanded by His Majesty George VI to invite you to preach at the parish church of Crathie on Sunday, August 27, 1939. . . ." Enclosed was a card inviting me to spend the weekend at the castle. Since the king had returned to London because of the crisis, I expected to hear any day that my visit was canceled. But no such message came, and on the Saturday before the big event I departed, suitably attired in frock coat and tall hat, bringing with me a suit of clerical evening dress that cost me all of ten pounds (and that I am able to boast I can still wear on suitable occasions). Queen Elizabeth (now the Queen Mother) was a radiant and graciously informal hostess. I was relieved to find that the prime minister had canceled his appearance, and there

89

were very few guests. At dinner I met John Elphinstone, the queen's nephew, whom I met again in the most dramatically different circumstances: we shared a pot of jam, the only meal of the day, in a dirty factory in Belgium on our march to Germany as prisoners of war. After church the next day I spent a riotous time with two little princesses (the present queen and her sister Margaret), aged fourteen and nine, playing kick-the-can in the garden. Before I left, the queen told me that she had been on the telephone to the king and had given him the text of my sermon. I mention this because the text I chose for that occasion was one I lived with for many years after that—Psalm 61:2: "From the end of the earth will I cry unto thee, when my heart is overwhelmed: lead me to the rock that is higher than I." Next Sunday we were at war.

My enrollment as a reserve chaplain meant a telegram on September 1 commanding me to proceed to Netley Hospital, near Southampton, to assume the responsibilities as chaplain to No. 11 General Hospital. That was the beginning of my undistinguished military career, and immediately I learned two things: one, the strange ways of the army, which I believe are internationally recognized; and two, the salutary lesson that I was not nearly as important as recent experiences were beginning to tempt me to believe. I arrived at Netley expecting to be shown to No. 11 Hospital and assigned to my room and office. But I found only the imposing hospital building (which dates back to the Crimean War), and nobody in it had ever heard of the hospital I had been assigned to. Eventually I met an old Scottish doctor of World War I vintage who informed me that he was second-in-command of No. 11. He told me that we were due to cross over to Le Havre in two weeks, that the present complement of the unit was one electrician and a couple of orderlies—and that I might find a bed in a vacant ward.

The next day I went up to London and visited Moss Brothers, the military outfitters. I emerged from the store resplendent in a captain's uniform and a cap with a chaplain's badge. There I was, with no training whatever in a chaplain's duties, no inkling of what to do next, and a vague idea that some time we would indeed embark for France. As I went up

Whitehall Street I heard a sudden crash. I jumped, then realized that a sentry was saluting me. I nearly raised my hat. I made my way back to Netley during a blackout (my first), thinking how different life had suddenly become. I was still a minister of the Kirk—or was I becoming something else?

The next day was Sunday, September 3, and Britain was still waiting for Hitler's reply to our ultimatum. Since the prime minister was to speak late that morning, I decided to go to the local church a little late. At eleven o'clock Big Ben boomed out the hour on the radio, and then Chamberlain announced that we were at war. I went to church with a strange jumble of thoughts and emotions and listened to one of the worst sermons I have ever heard, made worse still by the fact that the preacher hadn't bothered to discover that war had been declared. (That taught me a lesson on the importance of checking on current events before mounting the pulpit.)

Eventually my unit did indeed cross over to Le Havre, where during the ensuing months of the "Phony War" I decided that I would have been doing the Lord's work more effectively back home in the parish. Just before I left Coldstream to join the army, I had been called to Greenbank Church in Edinburgh, and as the months slipped by I began to consider dropping out of an army that didn't seem to be needed in this curious kind of war and beginning my second ministry. My only official duties were to attend to the needs of the few soldiers who had retired to our hospital (the Casino at Le Havre), although I soon discovered that there was an opportunity to fulfill my ministry by conducting services wherever there arrived a new unit of the rapidly expanding British Expeditionary Force. On Sundays I found myself in many curious places, often conducting six or more services for a curious mixture of men, from grizzled veterans to recruits as bewildered as I.

That winter was a strange one, a curious anticlimax after the apocalyptic visions we had had of a devastating head-on collision with the Nazis. Of course, it was good for me to be stripped of the protection of a country parish and the society of like-minded friends and plunged into the rough-and-tumble of army life. It was good for me to have to scrape together a congregation wherever I could find one and not just walk into a settled church situation every Sunday morning. And it was good for me to be thrown together with a group of people, mostly men with medical training, who showed little interest in theology and still less in the doings of the Presbytery of Jedburgh and Kelso. I realized how shielded I had been from the interests and the passions—not to mention the language—of the average British citizen of 1939. It did not take me long to realize that the twenty-minute sermon, carefully typed out word by word, was going nowhere with the men I was addressing in wards, cafés, dock-sheds, and barns. I didn't jettison all my theology and homiletic ideals, but I did realize that the communication of the gospel demanded a much wider experience of life in all its variety, and that the way Jesus spoke on the street corners or at the lake shore was much more appropriate to my situation than the conventional sermon delivered to the faithful on 'Sunday morning. On the other hand, this experience had its temptations. All in all things were far too easy for me. The life of an officer is an ambiguous one for a chaplain. When there is no fighting going on, its privileges can outweigh its responsibilities, and I don't think it was really good for me to be enjoying what was, on the whole, a much softer life than my wife and I had had in the manse at Coldstream. Apparently God agreed, for he soon arranged a dramatic change of environment for me.

At the beginning of 1940 I decided that I should at least get nearer to whatever action there might be, so I applied for a transfer to the 51st Highland Division, in which my father had served in World War I. In March I was given leave to return home for two weeks, and I seized the opportunity to have myself installed as minister of Greenbank Parish in Edinburgh. On that occasion I remember preaching about the story of Joseph, who found himself transformed from the favorite son of an indulgent father to a slave being marched to a prison in Egypt. The text was his words to his brothers— who were responsible for his misfortunes—at the end of the story: "But as for you, ye thought evil against me, but God meant it unto good." I told my new flock that whatever evil lay in wait for us, God could turn it into good. I didn't realize how soon that belief would be put to the test.

When I returned from my leave I found instructions to join the 51st Highland Division on the Belgian frontier. The telegram was full of army mumbo jumbo because no one was supposed to know where that division was. Since there was still no war being fought, I took my time getting there, traveling via Paris. There an old French gentleman presented me with a pipe he had carved out of cherry wood, thus launching my lifelong career as a pipe smoker; I ought not to commend it but I would be dishonest to regret it. After shuttling about from base to base, at one of which I learned the news that the Germans had suddenly pounced on Denmark and Norway, I tracked down my division near Lille and was shown into an officers' mess. I was told I could find the Deputy Assistant Chaplain General there. I found him, all right, but he was sound asleep in a big armchair. I waited patiently for half an hour, then coughed gently. He opened one eye, sat up, and asked, "Who the hell are you?" That had been my story since I had been drafted. Instead of being the up-and-coming young minister who had published two books and had a visit to Balmoral under his belt, in the real world of the army I was just one of many unknowns.

The DACG was a remarkable man. (I once heard him carry on two conversations simultaneously on two telephones, one in English and one in French.) After reprimanding me for my dilatory journey from Le Havre, he sped me off to join the RASC of the division; I spent some hectic months as their pastor before we were swept up in the grim events of June that year. We left the Belgian frontier to come under the command of a French corps deployed on the Maginot Line. The Scandinavian campaign was over, and we waited tensely for the next blow to fall. It was obvious that the Maginot mentality reigned in the French army, and that the World War I pattern reigned with the British. We were all set up with front-line trenches, casualty-clearing stations, rear lines, and base, ready for a 1914-like offensive—if indeed it came at all. I went up to the front line one day and saw that the Germans had spread out a huge banner a few feet in front of their trenches, which were a few yards away. "Français, ne tire pas," it read, "et nous ne tirerons pas." ("Frenchmen, if you don't shoot, we won't shoot.") The French shrugged their shoulders and said "Drôle de guerre." Any attempt by our general to provoke action was frowned on. And so we sat by the Maginot Line, waiting for something to happen.

It happened, all right. One morning shortly thereafter I heard the report on the radio about the Germans' overwhelming onslaught on Holland and Belgium. During the next few days we learned the names of the ill-fated places. Fort Eben Emael, a supposedly impregnable bastion on the Belgian frontier, had been taken by parachute troops. Some of the names I recognized from my father's discussions of the key points to the capture of the channel ports and the defense of Paris—Sedan, Arras, Amiens. Places that had been fought over for years in World War I were falling like ninepins. Soon came the incredible news that the Germans had surrounded the B.E.F. and had captured all the channel ports except Dunkirk. So there we sat, isolated from all our compatriots, hearing the dismal yet somehow inspiring news that most of the B.E.F. had been successfully evacuated, though it had lost all of its equipment. The BBC came through loud and clear with the news of the rescue, and Lord Haw-Haw (as we called the radio propagandist from Germany) droned on about the imminent surrender of France and the total isolation of Great Britain.

We got orders to move. Moving mainly at night, we circled around 1914 battlefields, traveling northeast to join in the defense of Paris. My war had begun at last, but it was still almost like a curious tour through some lovely parts of France; the only sign of war was the occasional appearance of a German plane completely unmolested by either the French or British air forces. We billeted in some beautiful country homes. I conducted services wherever I could, and talked strategy with my friend the medical officer. I even taught him to play chess. I remember that because on one occasion I explained what it means to sacrifice a pawn. "You allow the pawn to be taken," I said, "in order to improve your general position." Then, as an afterthought, I added, "Wouldn't it be funny if at this moment the British government was saying, 'There's that 51st Division. Let's sacrifice it so that we can claim that the U.K. is still fighting with the French.' " In fact, that was almost exactly what was happening, and in a week or so we were lined up along the Somme facing a regrouped German army poised to pounce on Paris.

As German planes came nearer to our units, I began hearing hair-raising stories from our troops about being shot up on the road. One sunny afternoon, just before we arrived at our positions, the medical officer and I were having a quiet drink in the garden of a lovely little chateau when he mentioned these tales. "I expect they mostly dreamed them up," he said. Just as he spoke, a Messerschmitt swooped low over our heads and fired a burst directly at us. The plane was so close that I could see the pilot's face. As my friend emerged from the illusory shelter of a rosebush, I emerged from another with the retort, "What was that you said?" Rumor had it that we were going to stage a minor Dunkirk of our own by withdrawing to Le Havre, where I had started my war in France, but it was soon obvious that we would have to move fast. Suddenly we heard that the Germans were around us, that Rouen had fallen and the Germans would get to Le Havre before we would. What we didn't know at the time was that the German general opposite us was Erwin Rommel, "the Desert Fox."

The coast of Normandy between Le Havre and Dieppe is lined with very high cliffs with little fishing villages and seaside resorts nestling among them. One of these is St.-Valery, the charms of which are described in a delightful book by Cornelia Otis Skinner and Emily Kimbrough called *Our Hearts Were Young and Gay*. (We read the book later in prison camp with mixed emotions!) We spent a day on a farm about a mile from St.-Valery waiting for orders that never came. We had no idea what was happening, and there were only muffled sounds of firing and the occasional bomb to disturb a beautiful June day. Having traveled slowly through the darkness all night, most of us just slept. When I woke I searched the farmhouse for books and settled down with Steinbeck's *Of Mice and Men*, which I read straight through without pause. The lunacy of the book seemed to match the lunacy of what was going on—or not going on—all around me. Then, in the evening, when rumors flew that we had to descend to the village, I gathered all the men within reach and held a short service in one of the fields. "My table thou hast furnished/In presence of my foes"—Scottish troops know the metrical version of the Twenty-third Psalm by heart, and it seemed particularly appropriate then. At the close of the service a young officer said to me, "Thanks, padre; I always say there's nothing like a spot of religion in a tight corner." I confess to having quoted that in sermons as an example of a popular attitude toward religion, but at the time I took it as a genuine expression of faith and gratitude.

When the orders came, we were sent off in little groups of about twenty to find our way to St.-Valery. Then began my twenty-four-hour experience of real war. Because it was so short, I hesitate to describe it when millions—from those who fought in the trenches in 1914 to those who fought in the jungles of Vietnam—have had an infinitely more prolonged and savage experience of warfare. All I can do is record my reactions as one of those who believed that war was sin but who also deeply believed that to have refused—in this crisis of human history—to resist the horrors of Nazism would have been a greater sin. Now I had, at least briefly, to face the consequences. War was no longer a word to be used in a sermon. It was that young Frenchman lying by the side of the road, killed by a bomb. It was peasants limping through the fields seeking shelter. It was burning houses and terrified children. It was two groups of young men—men with similar backgrounds, with wives and children, and often with similar religions—men who at home, as we say, wouldn't hurt a fly, aiming and firing at one another and hurling explosives that tore into human flesh like burning splinters of steel. I had read about it all in books. The reality was something else, but I'm not pretending that there and then I began to revise my views about "standing up to the Nazis" or the legitimacy of war in extreme conditions. Frankly, I was too concerned at the moment about saving my life and that of those around me, of whom—God help them—I was in charge. In the confusion that reigned as we descended the steep hill leading to the village, no one asked what a British officer wearing a clerical collar was supposed to be doing. French officers would dash up to me and give orders in fluent French. I hadn't time to explain that, although I understood their language, I knew nothing at all about military tactics or the firing of a "75." One of our officers came roaring up the hill announcing that the Germans were in the village and that we should make for Veules-les-Roses, a little fishing port a couple of miles away. The few who took his advice made the right choice. Most of them got home.

As we neared the village the confusion got even worse. The next thing I knew, a French officer ordered me to defend an orchard. In response I carefully placed my twenty men at intervals around the inside of the enclosing wall, since I had not the slightest idea whom to expect or from what direction. In the village, houses were burning; stray shots came from rooftops; horses galloped around at random. For what seemed like hours nothing happened. When someone competent appeared to defend my orchard, I took off with my group and went through the village to the harbor. On the way a French officer demanded that I interrogate a French soldier who claimed to have been captured and sent back to us with a message from the German general. The message, he told me, was that unless we surrendered by nine p.m., he would blow us all to blazes—or words to that effect. "We think that this man is a spy," the French officer told me. So I fired off a few questions to him in French and then quickly switched to German. He kept on answering. Fortunately, before reporting this, I asked another question: "Where is your home?" His reply—"In Alsace"—explained why he knew both languages, and I so reported.

My memory of the next few hours is somewhat cloudy. What I remember next is being on the edge of a dock. Suddenly there was an almighty roar, and the shells came hurtling in. I dived over the dockside into the mud with those around me and then looked at my watch. It was exactly nine o'clock. In the next ten minutes we got a painfully clear view of what a modern bombardment can do to a town in so short a time.

I passed around a small bottle of Calvados that I had bought for the mess, and we waited. When the firing stopped we climbed out of the mud, and then were given orders to move to a temporary headquarters that had been set up in a surviving hotel. I climbed up to a room where our general, Sir Victor Fortune, was quietly and confidently issuing orders for embarkation, as if we were catching the cross-channel ferry. Soon we were marching down a shattered street to the beach, dreaming somewhat skeptically of home.

Unfortunately, at the end of the street there were houses burning so vigorously that we couldn't get through. We soon realized that we couldn't go by the other end, either, since that was now ablaze, too. Then followed the most concentrated few minutes I have ever spent. Since I knew about the German general's message, I calculated that if he and his men repeated their earlier show of punctuality, they would almost certainly give us another dose at ten o'clock. The street was packed with troops. I remember that an old French woman made her way through the crowds of us, looking as though she had seen this sort of madness before and was ready for the worst. I caught sight of a little dog, and a question flashed through my head: Why should he suffer because of human cruelties? But the immediate question was the next salvo. We were trapped. Dr. Johnson said that the knowledge that one is going to die in a fortnight "concentrates the mind wonderfully." My mind was never so concentrated on the question of life and death as it was during those five minutes. As a chaplain, I did my best to look serene, but I was, of course, as terrified as anyone else. I discovered that the theology on which I had built my life got wonderfully simplified and concentrated. A whole mass of doctrines that I had considered of major importance seemed to winnow down to one person— Jesus Christ, crucified and risen—and the word that sounded in my soul was a verse from Saint Paul: "My God shall supply all your needs according to his riches in glory by Jesus Christ." There was a kind of peace that came with those words, not the peace that miraculously makes one want to shout "Hallelujah!" but one that seems to say, "That's it. I don't know what's going to happen. I don't know what the other side of death will look like. But I do know that God will supply all my needs."

Exactly at ten o'clock the clifftops were alive with flashes, and there was a roar of artillery. As we crouched down I noticed that every shell was passing over our heads and exploding on the beach. I still believe that in this instance I owe my life to General Rommel, who had obviously given the order to concentrate on any soldiers making for the boats and spare the troops trapped in the town. The sea was full of little boats, and one by one I saw them hit and sunk. As dawn came we were still huddled in the street, half asleep. But soon after that the fires that had trapped us died down, and we crept onto the beach, hugging the base of the giant cliffs. In the distance we could see Veules-les-Roses, where a Dutch freighter had been beached and was being boarded by our troops. My colonel told me to take twenty men and make for the boat. We crept along under the cliffs, where many victims of the bombardment lay strewn about. I found my friend the doctor, wounded. We had him carried back to a café on the beach, then continued our attempt at escape. Halfway along we came to a gap in the cliffs, and I noticed that the Germans had it covered. So we sat on ledges and waited. Any who tried to cross the gap were caught in the mortar fire. Then, to our horror, we saw the Dutch freighter hit amidships and blown to pieces. Meanwhile, back in St.-Valery, the last shots were being fired by our division, and the French general had surrendered. So I soon spotted a party of three coming along the beach with a white flag—two British soldiers and a German. A passing French soldier stopped and said, as if giving me instructions on how to get into a football match, "Il faut dire: 'Wir haben keinen armen.' " ("You must say: 'We haven't any arms.' ") Since that was true of me, I thought it was my duty to go out to meet the advancing party. The Frenchman grinned and presented me with a water bottle that I discovered was filled with rum. As soon as I appeared in the open, a German on the clifftop fired at me. I experienced that curious reaction of novices in war, the absurdly indignant thought "That fellow is actually trying to kill me." I now believe he wasn't, because every time I stopped and the advancing German beckoned me on, he fired again, and this curious waltz of captive to captor probably amused him greatly.

The young man to whom I formally surrendered was polite—and, as I now realize, extraordinarily kindhearted, because I began using all the German invectives I commanded to denounce Hitler for his invasion of Holland, Belgium, and France. I even referred to the previous violation of Belgium's neutrality in 1914. Later I learned from other prisoners that this feeling of rage was very common. The army teaches you that you may well be killed, and prepares you for the experience of being wounded. But nobody ever mentions that you might be taken prisoner—at least not during training. Though he might easily have clubbed me over the head, my captor simply asked quietly, "Rauchen Sie?" ("Do you smoke?") When I drew out my Frenchman's cherry-wood pipe, he grinned and pointed to the water. There, bobbing around on the waves, were hundreds of sealed cans of British tobacco. I took the hint and filled my uniform with as many cans as I could stuff in it. They kept me and four pipe-smoking friends going for at least half of our 250-mile trek to Germany. (This combination of French and German generosity, I confess, made me a confirmed pipe-smoker.) I was then directed to return to the St.-Valery beach and join my fellow prisoners. When I reached the café where I had left my doctor friend, another scene in this tragicomedy of war was enacted. The café was filled with wounded on stretchers, and a doctor and an orderly were giving first aid. I found my friend, who told me that he had been hit in the knee but otherwise felt all right. (I found another chaplain there whose wound was much more serious, and who subsequently died.) Those with minor wounds were sitting up and chatting when suddenly a French waiter popped up from behind the bar, asking for orders as if it were a normal June morning on the beach. I ordered champagne all around, and when I went to pay for it, the waiter told me, "The German general has ordered that all drinks are free today." So we had our drinks on Rommel, and I awaited the next step in this drama, which had the elements of farce.

I was soon directed up to the clifftops, where the remnants of our division were being assembled. As I passed through the village square, I caught a glimpse of our general being shown courteously into a car and being saluted by a German who must have been Rommel. (General Fortune became an inspiration to the rest of us during the five years we were in Germany.) It was a brilliant June day, and when I wandered to the edge of the cliffs it was so clear I could imagine seeing the coast of England. A group of Rommel's panzer troops stood on the edge of the cliff. Someone had told them that the man with the "dog collar" spoke German, so they wanted an interview. I remember the conversation distinctly. They were not ugly or threatening—just a group of young men on top of the world, thrilled to be standing on the channel coast which they had reached in a few weeks, the very place that for four years their fathers had fought and died for in a vain attempt to reach. They had three questions.

"You declared war on us, right?"

I had to agree. We were allied with the Poles, so we had had to issue an ultimatum when Poland was invaded.

"You didn't think we were so strong?"

I reflected on all the silly stories about cardboard tanks and dummy airplanes. "Perhaps," I answered.

Then came the clincher. "How long is this war going to last?"

There flashed through my mind stories my father had told me of how the Germans always feared a long war. "Years," I said. "Years and years."

They were not angry. They roared with laughter. "Fifteen days!" they all shouted. "Fifteen days—England kaput!"

I refrained from asking "und Schottland?" and simply pointed to the shining waters of the Channel. "How are you going to get over there?" I asked.

They knew the answer: "Flugzeuge!" they shouted. "England raziert." ("Thousands of planes. England will be razed to the ground.")

I shrugged my shoulders and rejoined my friends.

I'm trying to remember just how I felt—and why. I did realize that we were in for a long war, although if anyone had said "five years," some of us might have jumped over the cliffs. I could not believe that Britain would come to terms with Hitler. I genuinely believed that we would win, but I had seen enough of the German war machine to know what we were up against. And although these German soldiers were wearing belts with the inscription "Gott mit uns," I felt that, for once, surely it could be claimed that what we were fighting for was the possibility for the survival of Christian values, however poorly we had represented them in recent years. So it was with a combination of sheer hereditary pride and a real Christian conviction that I began the trek toward the unknown lot of a prisoner in Germany.

The France I loved was disintegrating before my eyes. But as we began to slog across the long roads that led through Flanders, Belgium, and Holland to the Rhine, I noticed that although the French soldiers were utterly dispirited and broken, the women who came out from their houses to watch us pass thrust bread into our hands, risked curses to bring us water, and whispered words of hope. And I remembered that for years I had noted that it was the women in France who had kept the faith, attending church and praying. So we kept step, braced ourselves, and sang whenever we went through the towns and villages. Along the way, tanks kept streaming past us, headed in the opposite direction. Hitler had said "Paris by June 15," and so it was to be. The whole parade of the Thousand Year Reich seemed unstoppable. One day a soldier leaped from his tank when we were resting in a village and, spotting my collar, came over and said, without malice but with the air of one stating an incontrovertible fact, "Your days are over. The Church is finished. We are in a new world."

Like all prisoners, we began to live in the land of rumor. The navy had sunk an invading armada; the Turks were coming into the war; the Americans were coming into the war; the French were building a new army in Algeria. But more important for us then was the daily report: We're about to reach the railhead. That meant making the rest of the journey in cattle trucks, although that prospect began to seem more and more desirable. But, like the other rumors, this one began to fade as no railhead ever appeared. We were doomed to march to Germany.

I began thinking about the way that God had led me

during the past year. Twelve months before, my wife and I had motored along some of these roads. Then there had been the call to a new church; then a broadcast, the publication of two books, and a visit to Balmoral; then the life of an army officer, with some ministerial duties, in virtual peacetime. Now I was nothing but one of over a million prisoners who tramped the roads of France. In a single moment a prisoner loses everything except the clothes on his back. Yet, as one friend later observed, "It takes losing everything to find one-self facing God." I was near the depths of despair. My wife, who was running a church hut in Rennes, was still in France. Would she get out? I knew the last possible port was Saint-Nazaire—and one day I grabbed a paper as we passed through a town and saw a photo of a big hospital ship lying sunk in that port.

A wise old colonel came alongside me one day on the march. "Padre," he told me, "your work is just beginning." He was right.

Chapter Eight

AN
ULTIMATE
GRACE

"He came to himself." That's what happened to the prodigal son in Jesus' story. He had run through his money, his possessions, his friends, and his hopes. There was nothing left but himself. And it was then that he thought about returning to his father.

Being taken prisoner means being stripped down. Suddenly everything you have come to rely on is gone. Your possessions, your job, your plans, those dearest to you, your country—all these are, in a peculiar way, no longer there. There's just you—and God? People often ask if prisoners naturally turn to religion. I think many do, just as people would fill the churches today if they lived in a city that was under the threat of immediate nuclear attack. But it's also true that hunger and thirst can drive almost every other thought from the mind. I had a little Greek Testament with me when I was captured, and I read it on the road. But a friend marching beside me remarked one day that he didn't see me reading it when we were passing through a village where French women were thrusting bread into our hands as we passed. Still, the experience of being stripped of all the other things on which one normally relies does throw one back on God in a very challenging way. Is he really there? Does he care about what's happening? All the texts on which one has preached—"God is our refuge and our strength," "Fear thou not, for I am with thee," "Your heavenly father knoweth what you need," "Seek ye first the Kingdom of God"—these suddenly seem either mere pulpit rhetoric or the most important words in the world. I knew then and ever after that they are real—even when the darkness falls and the foundations quiver.

Later, when we were in a prison camp, one friend told me that it was the experience of being stripped down like this that made him think seriously about God for the first time in years. He had been a stockbroker in London and described to me what his life had been like—commuting every day to his job, playing golf on weekends, enjoying his family and friends. As he put it, he "had no time for religion," and although he had had a conventional upbringing, church had just dropped out of his schedule. It was the "coming to himself" at the time of capture that changed his mind about the values of life. He never missed a service in camp, and when I last heard of him he was an elder in the Presbyterian Church. Similar things happened to others I got to know, but it would be false to imply that the experience of being prisoners automatically made men religious. When we had settled into the camps and adjusted to the new way of life, and when Red Cross parcels began to arrive regularly, another routine was established, and the proportion of believers to unbelievers, of practicing Christians to the indifferent, became roughly similar to what we had known at home. A cynic once remarked to me that the attendance at our church services was inversely related to the number of parcels arriving in the camp. When they came steadily, the number of worshipers dropped; when they faltered or ceased, the attendance rose.

The march from Normandy to Germany was a new experience for those of us who had enjoyed happy vacations in France and the Low Countries. Each day we were on the road by six A.M., five abreast in what looked like an endless column stretching along the flat roads as far as the eye could see, and we walked until nightfall with only occasional rests. There was no food in sight, and coffee and tea were just distant dreams. As we went through the villages there was always a chance of a crust of bread from the generous French women—

to be shared among five of us. (My partners always put me on the outside of the row, thinking that my clerical collar attracted more alms.) At noon we would arrive at the day's destination, usually a field where some elementary cooking and washing facilities had been set up. At that point, if you had the energy to join a line, a wait of two or three hours might win you a spoonful of soup. On some days there was no food at all. I once tried grabbing a huge turnip from a field we were passing, but a few bites were enough—and not worth the pangs that followed. Most nights we slept in the grass, and I discovered that the occasional downpour could be quite refreshing on the warmer evenings. As time went on we occasionally spent a night on a factory floor, and once in Tournai in Belgium we had the luxury of two nights in a civilian jail. I think it was here that I first heard the favorite reply of German authorities to any complaint about accommodations: "Hier ist kein Luxux-hotel!" ("This is no hotel deluxe.")

When someone asks how we were treated, I have to answer that on the whole the German army, at this point in the war, showed discipline and some respect for army traditions in their treatment of prisoners of war. We were not subjected to the brutality that prisoners suffered in the Far East then and since. Nor were we—on the march or in camp—victims of the appalling conditions prevalent in the concentration camps. Until Himmler took over in 1944, the German army paid at least minimal respect to the provisions of the Geneva Convention, and it was obvious to us that being in the hands of the army was totally different from being at the mercy of the Gestapo or any other of the Party organizations. Our guards on the march were not brutal. The semi-starvation we suffered was the result of the unexpected collapse of the Allied Forces. There were over a million prisoners on the roads at this time, and the problem of feeding them was enormous. My worst memory is of one blazing hot day when I was desperately thirsty. As we marched I saw a French woman ahead who approached the column with a large bucket of water. I kept my eye on that bucket as it got nearer and nearer. Then, just as I reached it, a guard kicked it over and the water drained away. In retrospect I realized that this wasn't quite as vicious an act as it seemed. Within a short time we arrived at our destination, where water was provided, and I suppose he was just trying to maintain order in the ranks. Seeing the enemy's point of view is not counted a military virtue, but the Apostle Paul showed signs of doing so when he was escorted to Rome as a prisoner.

We trudged along through Flanders, where the names of cities evoked memories of World War I, going straight on through Belgium and then Holland up to the banks of the Rhine. We usually observed Sundays with an informal service to which our captors made no objection. Whenever we were taken through a town, we British prisoners always straightened up, marched in step, and sang as lustily as we could. We discovered that we were allowed to sing everything from "Roll out the Barrel!" to the Twenty-third Psalm—with one curious exception. Our captors could not endure the sound of "Tipperary." They seemed to know that for us it meant a distant victory that would surely come again. The Rhine gave us a wonderful opportunity to remove our uniforms and take our first bath in three weeks. After that we were herded on-board barges and riverboats.

A few years before I had taken the Rhine trip in luxury, so at least I knew where I was. This time conditions were different. It seemed to me that we were lying two-deep on the deck, and since by this time many of us were suffering from mild dysentery, the prospects were not bright for a pleasant cruise into the heart of Germany. After a restless night I watched the dawn break and recognized the town of Dordrecht. The view around me was as depressing as our prospects. As far as the eye could see the river was crammed with barges full of British prisoners, although hardly a sound emerged from the morning mists. Then I noticed two figures standing by the dock to which our boat was tied. One was a large and genial Dutch civilian with a big cigar in his mouth. Beside him was a Germany sentry with a rifle and a fixed bayonet. Suddenly the strange silence was broken by a cockney voice from one of the barges. "Hi! Dutchie—'oo's going to win this war?"

The Dutchman removed the cigar from his mouth, expelled the smoke, and answered in a gruff voice, "England, of course!"

A loud cheer went up from the barges, and the sun broke through the mists.

We disembarked inside Germany and spent two foodless days in a barbed-wire pen before being herded onto trains to be shipped to our assigned camps. What I remember about this place was pacing around inside the wire with two majors from my division arguing about the future of the war. One of them belonged to the "home by Christmas" school. Since the other couldn't see that happening short of some compromise with Hitler, the argument was getting fierce. Suddenly a German sentry perched above us at his machine-gun post finished his breakfast and threw the crust of his sandwich into our pen. I pounced on it quick as lightning. We crouched beside a stone and measured that crust into three exactly equal parts, which we consumed like gourmets attacking a perfect filet mignon. It wasn't the last time that I was to reflect on how casually we accept the meals that come our way three times a day during peacetime, and how unreal are our occasional prayers of thanks. Later I got to know another major who was notorious in his camp for constantly talking about baked beans. His story was that he had been comfortably ensconced in a base hospital in France just as the Blitz began. He came down for breakfast one morning feeling somewhat cross and hung over, only to be confronted with a dish of baked beans his orderly had prepared. Properly enraged at being served such a dish for breakfast, he picked up the plate and threw it out an open window. That afternoon the German tanks arrived. He was rounded up and spent the next five years thinking about those beans.

Our first settled camp was at Laufen on the Salzach River, which flows between Germany and Austria. It had been the palace of the archbishops of Salzburg, but it was certainly no "Luxux-hotel." It might have comfortably accommodated a hundred people, but there were 1,500 of us—officers captured in every campaign from Norway to Dunkirk and St.-Valery. We were packed into rooms stuffed with three-tier bunks, each with a straw mattress. Some rooms had up to a hundred "guests," and as each of us had only heavy army boots to wear, the noise was endless both day and night. Food consisted of a loaf of bread to be shared by eight men, supplemented by a bucket of revolting soup twice a day. The soup was something you wouldn't give to a dog, but we counted the hours till it arrived. I began to learn still more about human nature and the leveling effect of hunger. I was in a small room with eight other chaplains. Comparatively speaking, these were luxury accommodations, a concession to our status as noncombatants who were supposed to be returned home as soon as possible. We had enough room for three three-tiered bunks, a table, and three chairs. We took turns going for the soup, and strict turns dishing it out. One day as this ceremony was underway, one of us leaped to his feet and shouted, "I can't stand it anymore! Here we are, nine ordained ministers of the Church of Jesus Christ, and we're all sitting here with our eyes fixed on that bucket to make sure that no one gets one teaspoonful more than we do." We knew it was true, and for a moment at least we were ashamed of how easily we had fallen into the great trap for every prisoner—ME FIRST! How many sermons on loving thy neighbor seemed to fall into that soup.

Before the Red Cross parcels began to arrive, life was dominated by thoughts of food—and also by a passionate desire to hear from home. At the same time we were preoccupied with the business of outwitting our captors, and the potential escapees soon got busy. Within a few months one tunnel had been constructed that was about a quarter of a mile long, running from under the stage where we had begun to put on shows to the Austrian side of the river. Among five hundred officers you are apt to find experts on everything— from chemists who know how to make dyes from herbs to turn a pair of pajamas into the field-gray of a German uniform, to mining engineers who know how to shore up and ventilate a shaft. Eventually this tunnel was constructed with hundreds of bed boards (each of us could sacrifice one without distress), and it was properly air-conditioned. Unfortunately, the tunnel was discovered, thanks to the activities of a German civilian expert who haunted our rooms and was known affectionately

110

as Horace the House Detective. But new plans kept sprouting. If I remember correctly, a professor of philosophy and an Oxford student were caught attempting to walk out disguised as the local chimney-sweeps.

In those early days we were the new boys, and the guards were fairly experienced. So when a search was conducted to discover contraband, the search party (which always swooped down unexpectedly and ransacked the camp) would triumphantly depart with quantities of maps, compasses, lighter fluid, rope, and other forbidden objects. (How these eventually got into the camps is another story about which an entire book could be written.) By 1943 or 1944 the situation was reversed. By then we were the experts. We had advance notice of upcoming searches, and we bribed the guards with cigarettes to mark our rooms as searched when they hadn't been inspected. On one such occasion the German officer in charge of the search party asked to see the senior British officer when it was all over. "I don't mind searching your camp and finding nothing," he said, "but could I please have my revolver back?"

The initial experience of prison life was dehumanizing. We were each given a number. I was *Kriegsgefangener* 1304. Because this was my identification for five years, it was graven on my mind. I had a photograph of myself at this time (subsequently confiscated) that showed me, with shaven head, holding a slate with my number on it. The shaving of the hair was meant to be a matter of hygiene, but it was extremely demoralizing for some reason. If you are having a theological argument with another chaplain, you are much more likely to lose your temper with him if he looks like a convict. God was cutting me down to size. A year ago I had been the bright young minister with prospects; now I was a number with a shaven head, one of thousands totally at the mercy of the Nazi powers.

There were thirty-one chaplains in the camp, and each reacted in a different way to the sudden change of environment. Each of us had had his little circle in which he was a spiritual leader, and now we were thrown together to live on scraps like everybody else. We had time to reflect on the remark that Studdert-Kennedy had made during World War I to the effect that chaplains were like manure: they did a great deal of good when spread thinly, but together in a heap they stank. Tensions inevitably developed, but two forces kept us from disintegrating as a spiritual force in the camp. One was a basic faith in Christ that held us together in spite of acute differences in denomination, theology, liturgy, and temperament. The other was a sense of humor. It was at this time that I learned that seeing the funny side of all that happens is not a minor compensation but one of God's greatest gifts of grace. I learned too that the Christians with the strongest faith were those who were best able to see the comic side of religion.

According to the Geneva Convention, chaplains and doctors were supposed to be repatriated by the first available route. Since that didn't seem to be about to happen, we protested against the policy of keeping all chaplains in an oflag (officers' camp) while leaving the men in the stalags without one. It was clear that the Germans preferred not to have anyone with an officer's rank in the stalags, but they assured us that repatriation would occur soon. Meanwhile, we took turns conducting services on Sunday, saying morning and evening prayers every day, and offering lectures and Bible studies. The enduring benefit for a minister of this kind of parish was the breaking down of the barriers that often separate the clergy from their flocks at home. This was life in a goldfish bowl. There was no possibility of a chaplain's having a public image that might be totally different from his real self. Nor could a chaplain live in any kind of splendid isolation. We endured the same living conditions, the same food, the same deprivations as everyone else. And we had the opportunity of rubbing shoulders with men who would hardly ever attend a church or meet a minister in civilian life. I felt as though God had said to me, "You've had a very limited experience of my great human family. You don't really know how many of them think, how they talk, and what you mean by the words you use when talking about me. So I've dropped you in at the deep end. Swim around and you'll learn more about human nature than you ever did at seminary."

As I've said, food was a major preoccupation. And so

were mail, tobacco, and books. Letters from home eventually arrived, and we were allowed to send a limited number of letters and cards to our families. Thus by Christmas I learned that my wife was safely home—if living in London and being bombed out of three apartments could be called "safe"—and at about the same time she learned that I was alive and a prisoner. Mail was, in short, a lifeline. (When, in 1943, I was in a camp selected for one of Hitler's reprisals and we were deprived of all mail for several months, we would willingly have starved again in return for the letters that were piling up in the *Kommandantur*.) Our original stores of tobacco had soon run out, but after six months supplies came from home, and soon we had enough cigarettes to bribe our guards. Books began to arrive, and we rationed them carefully, reading slowly and savoring every word—with one exception. We discovered that almost every book we opened began describing in detail the glorious meals the characters enjoyed. I never noticed this before nor have I since, but we used to toss down a book with the angry question "Why must these novelists keep talking about food?"

When Red Cross parcels finally began arriving, our lives were radically changed. These parcels were carefully designed to give us all the extra calories we needed, and they banished our obsession with food for the next few years. Of course, our stomachs had adjusted. New prisoners in the later years found our rations woefully short, but we answered their complaints with "Wait until the parcels stop." It was a good experience for us to be, for once, on the receiving end of what's called charity. Before America entered the war some privileged prisoners with friends in the States received private parcels that offered an interesting change of diet. (Once I remember seeing a friend of mine sitting at a table, carefully slitting open a succession of tea bags and pouring the contents into a jar. "What a damn funny way to pack tea," he remarked.)

When books were in short supply, lectures were a godsend. No one cared what the subject was so long as the lecturer was lively and interesting. I once attended a course on mercantile law simply because it gave me something new to think about. I taught some brief courses on theology, and got together a group to study the Epistle to the Romans, but what I remember most vividly is reading and expounding *Paradise Lost* to a chartered accountant, a wine merchant, and a regular officer. We worked our way through the entire piece. One of the chaplains, a New Testament professor from Cambridge, was overjoyed when I lent him my little Greek version, and he proceeded happily to expound it. But his chief gift to the camp was a series of lectures called "Historical Geography," a title devised to deceive the German authorities. For what he was offering was a military appraisal of the war situation. Military history was his avocation, and I remember well how he assessed the probable future course of the war. He was convinced that America would eventually join in and that in the end the Allies would be victorious. But he was decidedly unpopular with the "home by Christmas" thinkers. (Incidentally, that saying became a bad joke after it had been repeated for five Christmases—and I feared the worst when it was later used in Korea just before the Chinese intervention.)

On the lighter side, we were soon busy putting on concerts, plays, skits, and musicals. Since we had two or three West End theater directors and a number of actors in the camp, the productions were of professional quality. I have always enjoyed acting (every competent preacher has a streak of ham in him), so it was an education for me to learn of the discipline that goes into the production of even the lightest bit of farce. Our audiences were highly critical but appreciative. They especially enjoyed satire on camp life and subtle innuendos that slipped past the German censor, who was always present. Many years later, in another camp, a hardened veteran told me that he had always been grateful to me for what I did for him in Laufen. I waited for some tribute to a sermon I had preached and was surprised when he went on, "Yes; you were the first person who made me laugh." So be it.

Looking back, I see that God was in the laughter, and in a mysterious way he was leading us to a new understanding of human nature. When one is stripped of the veneer of customary civilities and the assurance that the necessities of life are readily available, there is a raw reality about relationships in which true religion flourishes, and the pretentious, the insincere, and the fanatical stick out like a sore thumb. The first shock was the realization of how utterly selfish human beings can be, including oneself. But that was followed by moments when one marveled at the sheer goodness, courage, and good humor one found in the kind of person ministers are inclined to write off as coarse and unspiritual. In these circumstances one's understanding of both sin and grace was enormously deepened. Since I was still under the influence of some of the evangelical movements I have described, it puzzled me to find that some of the most fervent believers behaved rather badly under the stress of hunger and anxiety, while those I would have considered somewhat lukewarm in what is called "Christian witness" were pillars of decency and goodwill. It began to dawn on me that those who were desperately concerned with the salvation of their own souls—whether they expressed this in evangelical or "High Church" terms—were also likely to be equally concerned with meeting their own physical needs. It is because of this experience that I have reservations about all religion that tends toward the fanatical and the demonstrative.

The one specter that began to haunt us over the years was the thought of an indefinitely extended imprisonment. We didn't talk about it, but it was there, and it is the only recurring nightmare I connect with my life as a P.O.W. We never contemplated defeat, but at times, as more and more countries got dragged into the war, it seemed like there could be no end to the stalemate. Already at Laufen it was clear to most of us that there were some years of confinement ahead, so we settled in and tried to make the best of it. We endured periods of boredom and an occasional wave of depression, but we learned to cope with these. Those of us who were chaplains and doctors, of course, were lucky, because we were able to continue our work in camp. Others eventually managed to prepare themselves for their professions by getting books from home to study. Some even passed examinations by mail. Those worst off were the regular soldiers, who saw their promotions frozen and their expertise in military affairs become rapidly out-of-date. Almost everyone was involved in one way or another with escape plans. News-gathering and rumor-evaluating became specialities in which I later played a part (when we had secret radios and got the BBC).

As I think back on sermons preached, I don't remember any constant harping on our own peculiar problems. They were like sermons at home, attempts to commend the gospel, explain the Bible, and build up faith—without promises and quick fixes. Religion was not a matter of spectacular conversions, ecstatic experiences, or emotional orgies; it was a solid trust in God and belief in Christ as the way, the truth, and the life.

Still, I do have a vivid memory of one mystical experience. It was an evening in the fall of 1940. Conditions were at their worst. We were getting very few letters; the potatoes on which we relied for basic sustenance had gone rancid; the war news was of victorious Nazi armies. I went out to walk around inside the wire by myself. On the way I passed the screaming headlines of the *Volkischer Beobachter* (the Party newspaper) plastered on the wall: "LONDON EIN EINZIGES FLAMMENMEER!" ("London is one sea of flames!") I knew my wife was there. Yet, a few minutes later, as I stood looking out over the river, I was overcome by an indescribable sense of peace and a strange joy, as if the angels were singing through the barbed wire and reaching deep inside me. I had heard of the fasting of saints and mystics, and I wondered if part of their secret was their physical hunger. I don't know how to account for my experience, and I am not ready to hand it over to either theologians or psychiatrists. It was real. But it didn't last, or even recur with the same intensity. Soon I was wandering back to the oflag—thinking about bread.

After eighteen months at Laufen—during which time the German army moved into Russia and Herr Hess made his celebrated solo flight to Scotland (we got a lot of fun out of that)—it was suddenly announced that chaplains and doctors were about to be repatriated. We were speedily herded onto a train and sent to Rouen in France. We were told that a boat was waiting at Le Havre, and we were to be exchanged for German prisoners on the Isle of Man. But it never happened. Negotiations broke down, and we spent an extraordinary winter on the racecourse of Rouen in a ramshackle but not too uncomfortable camp, in which I served as official interpreter. The local commandant with whom I had to conduct official business was a fine old gentleman, a devout Christian. He did his best for us, and those in our party who were badly wounded were grateful. On Christmas Eve they made him a huge Christmas card and asked me to deliver it to him at midnight. I still can see him standing there in his office, lighting the last candle on an Advent wreath. I handed him the card. He was an erect and soldierly figure. He and I both knew that we were trying to do our duty by our country. My job was to wring concessions from him, help in escapes, and boost the morale of our troops while depressing that of the German guards. His job was to keep us firmly under control and to prevent escapes. We were at war. Yet there in the light of that Advent candle, as the bells of Rouen pealed the midnight hour, he looked at the card and the tears ran down his cheeks. Instinctively we shook hands. And there was at least a moment's armistice in that horrible war as we wished each other a Merry Christmas. His name was Villaret, Hauptman Villaret.

The tragicomedy of our winter in Rouen could fill a book. There was the disappointment to deal with, the gradual realization that we were not, after all, headed for home. I shared that completely, and it's almost impossible to describe. But as chaplain I had the added responsibility of ministering to my colleagues and the thousand badly wounded who were waiting to return to the care of family and friends, and as camp interpreter it was my job to keep this curious group happy and hopeful by means of negotiations in German, French, and English. We also had to combat the cold. We were starved not for food but for fuel, and the devices we employed to obtain firewood were many, varied, and sometimes hilarious (as when, one night, we planned and executed the removal of the entire starting gate on the race course). Through maneuverings among the German officers, whose rivalries I learned, I got in contact with French civilians and discovered among other things that I could get French books smuggled, undetected, into the camp. I ordered a number of theological tomes which were duly delivered. With my next order I included a request for *Guide Bleu de la Normandie*, and to my surprise I got a copy, which contained splendid maps of the area.

That was the beginning of a series of escapes, culminating in the departure one night of a friend known as "Bloody Bob" and six Australians. The key figure of the whole episode, which took considerable planning, was a French girl of seventeen with whom I maintained a clandestine correspondence. I cannot forget her. She had everything to lose by her efforts, whereas our men were risking little but some temporary discomfort if they were recaptured. When, following Bloody Bob's instructions, I asked her what the exact plans were for their escape after getting out of the camp, she wrote back: "I know nothing of where you go beyond the first night. If you trust me, go through the wire at ten tomorrow night. You will be in Gibraltar in three weeks. If you don't trust me, call it off." They went. The wire-cutters she had obtained for us worked perfectly. All the men made it through except one, who got stuck in the wire and consoled himself by drinking half a bottle of brandy. When he was discovered, all hell broke loose, but between the nonsense the victim was talking and the deliberate mystifications in which I was indulging, it took the guards over an hour to take a head count in the camp. Thereafter, until I found myself being interrogated by the army's secret-service man, the evening was a riot of elation and confusion. Eventually all our boots were removed and we were locked securely in, and a few days later we were dispatched on a train to the Polish frontier. Before he had left, Bloody Bob had thanked me for the arrangements. "In a month I'll have lunch with your wife at the Savoy," he told me. Some time later, when I was in the heart of Germany, I received a letter that said: "You will be interested to know that yesterday I had lunch at the Savoy with a friend of yours called Bloody Bob." (The Germans were, of course, unaware of who this was.) We managed one more escape when we were leaving Rouen. As we went off to our train, we helped the surgeon and another officer hide in a hole under the stove in my room. They waited a couple of days and then set off with one of my precious maps. The surgeon got home and joined the party at the Savoy.

We were sent to the stalag of Lamsdorf in Silesia, not far from Poland. It was a new experience to be with thousands of British troops, and they were delighted to see us officers, however bedraggled and dispirited we were. We held huge services in one of the barracks and soon learned about the morale of the camp. The troops were invincibly optimistic and gave their guards a hard time. This was typical of every stalag to which I was sent: there was always a strange mixture of hostility and camaraderie between prisoners and guards. Fans of "Hogan's Heroes" will know what I mean when I say there was always a Schultz around—genial, good-humored, and the butt of constant practical jokes.

By this time we were pressing for the assignment of doctors and chaplains to the various camps. It was agreed that we could stay in stalags and oflags as camp chaplains if we gave up any right to repatriation. All except those who were physically unfit volunteered, and we waited for orders. I got orders, all right, but I was rapidly expelled from stalag after stalag, being suspected (quite correctly) of spreading propaganda designed to raise the spirits of our men and depress the guards. The result was that I spent some years in a little oflag in the village of Elbersdorf by the town of Spangenberg, about ten miles from Kassel.

I could write several volumes about life in Oflag 1X. This particular goldfish bowl had only two hundred very senior fish in it. We got to know one another as intimately as human beings ever can. That was where I was really trained as a preacher and pastor. Over the years I've remained close to the friends I made there—including the *Feldtwebel*, whose job was to run the camp and prevent escapes. I tracked him down after the war, and we spent an uproarious evening reminiscing in a hotel in Frankfort. He had a few questions to ask me, and I spilled out mine to him. Did he know about the tunnel? Did he guess that we had a secret radio? Who were those Gestapo agents who looked so meek and mild? And what happened to him after our people were marched out?

Eventually I said, "I want you to know that we found you a good soldier—too good for our purposes—and always fair."

He smiled. "I am so happy. I know you wouldn't have phoned me up unless that was true."

At Spangenberg I began a series of lectures on the Christian faith in collaboration with a Church of England chaplain. We tackled basic questions of belief, and soon the camp was in a turmoil. Since we all knew one another so intimately, everything was out in the open—beliefs, unbeliefs, and half-beliefs. We had all the time in the world to follow up the lectures with discussions that covered the whole ground of religion. Day after day we spent hours confronting two convinced and erudite atheists. We heard stories of church experiences, good and bad. We had to delve back into every theological book we had ever digested. Never again have I been forced to examine so thoroughly everything I profess to believe in, or to listen to such frank and sometimes devastating criticism. One day after we had concluded that series, the camp was searched. As we waited endlessly on the parade ground, I made an effort to reach a lavatory but was blocked by a German guard. We had a little argument which I eventually won, and he let me use the facilities. When I emerged he asked me if it was true that I had been giving lectures on the Christian faith. When I admitted it, he replied, "That interests me a lot. You see, I'm a Lutheran pastor and my church is in the neighboring village." That set us off on a long theological discussion while the rest of the camp patiently waited for the search to end. Eventually he told me, "I'm working in the censorship department at the *Kommandantur*. If you would like a copy of your lectures to be sent home, I could arrange it." I said that would be wonderful; perhaps a book could be made of them. Then he said, "If you give me your word as a Christian that there will be no code in the manuscript, I'll see that it goes off at once." I gave my word, and within a short time I heard from my wife that the manuscript had arrived and had been accepted for publication by the SCM Press. Shortly after that my friend was removed from the camp.

The sequel was interesting. In 1956 I was traveling through Germany visiting church leaders. I had a car at my disposal so I could go wherever I wished. One day I reached Spangen-berg, and I was immediately recognized by the villagers in Elbersdorf and treated to a feast of wine and apples. (When we had been P.O.W.'s there, the villagers, whom we saw through the wire every day, were friendly and as helpful to us as they could be. As thanks for their kindness, I had written to British authorities after the war and succeeded in having one of them repatriated from a British P.O.W. camp in Egypt.) When I inquired about the pastor, they offered to take me to him, and soon I was talking with my pastor-guard once again. I asked him what had happened after he left our camp. "I was sent to the Afrika Corps," he explained, "and within a month I was a prisoner of the British." He went on to say that he and the other P.O.W.'s had complained about having nothing to read and so received a crate of books via the YMCA. "And the first book I saw," he said, "was the one I sent home for you— *Prisoner's Quest.*" The book was eventually published in America, too, and *The Atlantic* printed a chapter of it. The editions were small, and I can't find any copies now. Those who did buy it expecting lurid tales of escapes must have been puzzled to find nothing but Christian apologetics.

After the great invasion on D day, an event we had awaited for years, the camp was seething with excitement. We affixed a huge map to the wall of our recreation room that showed our camp as the center of the world, carefully noting the battlelines approaching from the east and the west; we went strictly by the German communiqués that we had learned to interpret. The results were quite spectacular after the break-through in the summer and the rapid advance of the Russians from the east. "Home by Christmas" was at last a safe bet. Yet Christmas 1944 found the Allies not only stopped in their tracks but in mortal danger during the Battle of the Bulge. Never did I have a harder time conducting carol services and preaching a Christmas sermon. I was living on the belief that what happened at Christmas was joyful news for the world no matter what our situation might be. I wrote a scathing poem denouncing the current saying in the camp—"Let's not celebrate Christmas this year"—and in the end we did rejoice in our own way and found our spirits revived in spite of the disappointments in the news.

Another poem I had written earlier dealt with the fact that we were the spectators, selfishly concerned with our Red Cross parcels and our tobacco, while millions were dying in battle. I was listening to the BBC nearly every day and holding a news conference every afternoon, so I often heard the remark, "A dull communiqué." Hence this bit of doggerel:

NOUS AUTRES

STRETCHED in the sun, an idle finger flipping
The glib evasions of the Oh Kah Vay*—
A lazy voice emerges from the sipping
Of tepid beer: "Well, what's the news to-day?"
"Attacks repulsed; some tanks and planes and
  shipping;
Nothing at all: a dull Communiqué."

By Bjelgorod a thousand tanks are churning
The peasants' acres into crimson mud—
Mechanic genius of an age returning
To Mother-nature by the path of blood—
And this same sun, high over Etna burning,
Stares on the fury of invading flood.

A mile above the northern coast, a roaring
Of heavy bombers racing through the Flak:
Across their path a lonely fighter soaring
Drops like a dewdrop in a silver track:
Onward, like swans—but, snug beneath the flooring,
Pendent destruction on a flimsy rack.

Far out at sea a convoy slowly homing
Rides the Atlantic with a wary eye;
Restless destroyers diligently combing
Pounce to a message from the watching sky:
Soon on the waves a sullen oily foaming
Betrays the tomb wherein the U-boats lie.

*OKW, the German High Command of the armed forces

AN ULTIMATE GRACE

Inside the wire a nineteen-forty fighter
Removes his pipe and waves a wasp away:
"You must admit that things are getting brighter—
A box of matches every fifteenth day!
But what's the news?" "I've told you all, you blighter—
Nothing at all: a dull Communiqué."

As we reached the spring of 1945, the tensions increased. It was obvious that the Allies would be reaching our area within a few weeks; it was equally obvious that the Germans would move us out eastward at any moment. But already we were living "eschatologically"—that is, with a strong sense of the end being near, whatever that end would be. Then one day in March the senior British officer sent for me. A Swiss representative of the Red Cross was having a private interview with him, and he needed an interpreter. Soon the Swiss began to speak of a stalag about fifty miles away where about ten thousand men were living in appalling conditions. Some, like the French, had been in the camp since 1940. Recently about two thousand British prisoners had arrived after having been evacuated from camps in the east as the Russians approached. They had crossed Germany on foot under terrible conditions, he said, and some were already dying of exhaustion. He reported also that American prisoners captured in the Battle of the Bulge had appeared and were in bad shape. Food supplies were extremely low, and the commandant was a brute—"assassin" was one word he used to describe him. The sum of it was that the camp needed a doctor and a chaplain. Since we had two of each, a doctor and I volunteered to go.

As we left, our friends waved good-bye with a certain amount of foreboding about our fate. We were, however, going about fifty miles closer to the approaching American Third Army, and that was to lead to some real excitement.

After a slow and bomb-delayed railway journey, we arrived at Ziegenhain, where the camp was located. It was a bleak prospect, as if a pall of death hung over the place. "Abandon hope, all ye who enter here," muttered my doctor friend as we passed through the gates. I found a British sergeant major who was as smart and efficient as they usually are. He was astonished to see two officers who looked reasonably clean and healthy, and I explained why we were there. He found a two-tiered bunk for us in his quarters and told us to watch out for fleas and lice. He painted a grim picture of conditions in the camp.

"But the men are not giving up," he said; "they are betting on which of the three 'P's' will come first."

"What 'P's'?" I asked.

"Parcels, Patton, or Peace," he replied.

When I suggested that I should introduce myself to the commandant, he shook his head.

"You really want to see that swine?"

I pointed out that I had to get a pass from him to visit the British and American troops.

As I approached the commandant's office I could hear him yelling and screaming. One of the guards was on the mat and soon came out looking white and scared. When I informed another guard that I wanted to see the commandant, he looked at me as if I were crazy, then jerked a thumb toward the door of his office. Once in the commandant's presence I made my request after explaining that I had come to minister to British and American prisoners. He glowered at me, but he had obviously received some instructions about us. He wrote out a pass to the British compound, and I was about to argue for my rights to minister to the Americans when an air-raid siren went off. In a few minutes I found myself crushed beside him in a slit trench while Allied planes roared overhead. It was hardly the best atmosphere in which to continue our conversation, so I slipped away when the all clear sounded.

I held my first service on Palm Sunday, after having seen as many of our men as possible. Few of the British were able even to stand up; they were dying at a rate of about two a day. Naturally I wondered what sort of a response I would get. I found men in various stages of exhaustion and starvation but extraordinarily receptive to this curious pastoral visit. Never before or since have I found men of all types so ready to talk about God and to hear the story of Christ. "I've never been a religious man," said one of them, "but somehow on that march God was very real. What did that mean?"

As they lay on the ground I told the Palm Sunday story, stressing the way Jesus had "set his face" to go to Jerusalem, ready to endure whatever might happen to him there. I spoke of his sharing everything that had happened, or could happen, to us, and how God comes close to us in him. I spoke of the Easter that was a week away. I think all of us knew that by then we would be either free or dead. We prayed and managed to sing a verse or two of a familiar hymn. In a way far from the conventional sense of the words we knew we were "in the hands of God"—a real God. And in the presence of Christ and his Cross, no one asked me why we had been allowed to get into this situation.

During Holy Week the commandant decided to march us all out of the camp before the Americans could arrive. We could hear the sounds of the guns of the Third Army getting closer every day. Eventually we were ordered to go on parade, prepared to march out eastward. Few could even drag themselves out of the huts, and I searched out the commandant in order to protest the move. I think I managed to drop a hint about war crimes and coming retribution, because he suddenly relented.

"All right," he said. "*I* am going, and all who want to follow can join me."

To my surprise, most of the French lined up to go. I asked a Jesuit priest who was with them as a combatant soldier why they didn't wait for the arrival of the Americans.

"We've been here since 1940," he told me, "and we know that the camp is mined."

I thought that over. "I don't think the Germans would take the risk of blowing us all up," I replied—with perhaps a little more assurance than I really felt.

So the commandant set out with his volunteers, leaving a skeleton guard on duty. I summoned the leaders of all the national contingents, and we had a conference with the German officers who remained. We reached an agreement that they would remain on duty so that any inquisitive German units in the neighborhood could be told that all was in order. The Allied prisoners then took over the running of the camp inside. An American doctor and I were then in charge, though neither of us was really competent to organize a camp of ten thousand men of a dozen different nations and languages.

I had been given certain signals we could use to warn Allied airmen that this was a P.O.W. camp. This was extremely important, as we had been strafed a few days before and about forty of us had been killed. When Thursday night came, we gave orders for everyone to remain secluded in their huts. I walked down to the gate and found a courteous and reasonable German officer using his field glasses to look first to the east, then to the west. He informed me that the American army was in the nearest village. "But," he said anxiously, "there are S.S. up there in the woods." So we agreed that we would continue to play dead.

A couple of American soldiers came to tell me of an escape plan: they were going through the wire that night. I tried to dissuade them, but they were determined. The results were sad: both of them were shot by a jumpy guard, and conducting their funerals was my first job after liberation. I didn't sleep that night, and watched Good Friday dawn over a dreary but expectant camp. I decided to visit as many huts as possible. By noon I had conducted services in half a dozen places, and still there was total silence, east and west. There we were: Americans, British, French, Russians, Yugoslavians, Australians, South Africans, members of the Foreign Legion. I remember meeting them all and talking about the Cross. There was no more food, but we almost forgot about our hunger as we waited for the climax.

In the afternoon I went to the American compound. Inside the huts groups of Roman Catholics, Protestants, and Jews were saying prayers. I invited them to join me in a Good Friday meditation. For some reason I looked at my watch as I was speaking, and I remember saying, "It's three o'clock. This is the moment when Jesus died for the liberation of the whole world. Why don't we sing the Doxology?" As the strains died away I heard a noise outside. When I opened the door, I could scarcely believe my eyes. The entire camp was surging down toward the gates, cheering and shouting, and there were the American tanks roaring past, with men throwing us chocolate, cigarettes, and cans of beef. "You can come out now," I announced to my congregation, and we rushed down to the gate.

I saw an American officer walk in, the first free Allied soldier I had seen in five years. "Good afternoon, sir," I said. "I'm glad to see you—and that's an understatement."

"Gee," he replied, "and they say the British have no sense of humor."

I enjoyed other exciting moments before I found myself flying back over the cliffs of Dover, but that Good Friday lives in my heart. Just as Christ died to set sinners free, so we knew that millions had died to liberate us. We could do nothing but accept the gift and be grateful. We were in a daze; it didn't seem true. A young Scottish soldier came up to me and opened a Bible to Psalm 126. "When the Lord turned again the captivity of Zion," I read, "we were like them that dream."

Epilogue

It seems reasonable to break off these reflections at this point. There was, of course, more to come—more than half of my life—but 1945 was a turning point. Five years as a prisoner of war left their mark on me. It was not quite the same person who returned to civilian ministry.

As I look back in gratitude on the postwar years, it is clear that there was more grace to be given. It was given to me when I needed it to endure the agonies of readjustment (all of us found it hard to communicate with the "normal" world), and to reassess my task as a preacher. It was also given to me in the unexpected twists in the direction of my life, the first one leading me, wide-eyed and surprised, to the Madison Avenue Presbyterian Church in New York, which has been my challenge, love, and joy for over a quarter of a century now. I hope to write about all of this in the near future, once I can find a perspective from which to select the points at which God was shaping my course, changing my mind, and enlarging my understanding of the gospel I was committed to preach. Such reflections will surely include an assessment of the influence of the American mind and spirit on this cosmopolitan but die-hard Scot.

If a preacher is an individual with one hand stretched out toward God in faith and the other extended toward other people in understanding and compassion, then my experience as a P.O.W. surely helped me with that human touch. It was a postgraduate course in Christian anthropology, which is an elaborate way of saying that I learned more about human nature (including my own) at its highest and lowest points than I could ever have known in the limited circles to which a conventional ministry would have confined me.

A prison parish is with a minister twenty-four hours a day. It consists of every kind of person (except women), and everyone gets to know one another intimately. The chaplain shares the same quarters, eats the same food, and talks the same language as everybody else. A sermon, therefore, has to communicate—or no one will listen. In my prison parish our communication was direct and increasingly nonverbal. We dispensed with unnecessary talk. (The first thing I noticed on my return was the immense amount of useless chatter going on all the time.) Since then I have not experienced so close an identification with those to whom I preach, but I hope that some of this sensitivity to the mind and spirit of those who are not conventionally religious has remained with me.

When Paul wrote about grace being given to him "to preach among the Gentiles the unsearchable riches of Christ," these "Gentiles" represented for him a people totally different from those with whom he had associated as a "Hebrew of the Hebrews." For me the "Gentiles" are the vast number of those for whom conventional Christianity or Judaism has ceased to have a powerful appeal—perhaps has even become meaningless. The grace I seek is the ability to understand and then with compassion to interpret the gospel to all such people.

But it was not only this hand of the preacher that was sensitized in the prison camps. The hand that reached out to God for his Word found new and strange things given. The center held—Jesus Christ as Lord and Savior—but many religious beliefs and practices, many hasty judgments and prejudices were shaken up and winnowed in the sieve of prison life (and of such battle as came my way). Perhaps I will write about these as well, since they raise questions that many are asking today.

Meanwhile, let me end this part of one preacher's life with the confession that "living by grace" means more to me than ever as I gratefully try to be husband, father, preacher, and pastor in these dangerously fascinating times, and to welcome the years ahead. For whatever they bring, I know they will reveal the "unfathomable riches of Christ."